JIGSAWS

by

Jennifer Rogers

The Dramatic Publishing Company
Woodstock, Illinois • Wilton, Connecticut • Melbourne, Australia

*** NOTICE ***

Cover design by Susan Carle.
ISBN: 0-87129-016-2

JIGSAWS

A Play in Two Acts
For Five Women

CHARACTERS

EMMA .....a widow, about 70, mother of Sylvia and Pat
SYLVIA ....mother of Monica and Alex
PAT ....Sylvia's sister
MONICA ....Sylvia's daughter
ALEX ....her sister

SETTING: The lounge room of a suburban home in Perth, Western Australia

TIME: The present, covering a span of just over a year

Jigsaws was first performed by The Hole in the Wall Theatre company at The Hole in the Wall, Perth on 5 February 1988, with the following cast:

PAT	Sally Sander
ALEX	Lucinda Amour
EMMA	Margaret Anketell
MONICA	Leith Taylor
SYLVIA	Rosemary Barr

Directed by Jenny McNae
Designed by Serge Tampalini

ACT ONE

SCENE: *It is mid-afternoon on Christmas day. A late, long family lunch has just finished. The lounge room is furnished with old-fashioned, heavy furniture, and is decorated in sombre colours. It is a room which has not changed much over the past thirty years. There are two doors: one leads to the hall and bedrooms, the other out into the kitchen and back garden.*

The room is strewn with Christmas paper and empty glasses. The blinds are drawn and the curtains closed, shutting out the heat of the day. The radio is playing: Judy Garland singing "Have Yourself a Merry Little Christmas."

PAT is seated in front of a coffee table working on a jigsaw. She is having problems. The border has been done but little else. ALEX enters from the kitchen carrying a glass of wine. She is happily, though not obviously, intoxicated. She turns off the radio.

ALEX. Do you mind? I wondered how you'd managed to escape. Mum's still ordering the boys around, Monica's fighting with Chloe about who's going to wash up, Dad and Nick have gone back on the beer, and Aunty Nellie is bowling leg breaks on the back verandah. I knew there was some good reason why I hadn't been home for Christmas in five years. *(Looking over Pat's shoulder.)* I didn't know you liked jigsaws.

PAT. I hate them. Look at it. Ten thousand pieces and they're all the same colour.

ALEX. You've done the edge.

PAT. Chloe did the edge. In three minutes and twenty-six seconds. I timed her. She said: *(In a little girl voice.)* "What have I done, Aunty Pat?" So I told her what she'd done: the easy bit.

ALEX. Why torture yourself? If you don't enjoy it, don't do it.

PAT. Is that feminist philosophy?

ALEX. Just common sense. Are you going to ring Uncle Ken?

PAT. Why? I only left Sydney two days ago. The beer won't have run out yet.

ALEX. He's probably missing you dreadfully.

PAT *(laughing)*. And there's snow on the harbour bridge.

ALEX. Seriously. He couldn't tell you. You know how shy he is.

PAT. We're not talking about Bambi of the forest, are we? Uncle Ken is fifty-two years old. I don't even hold his hand when we cross the road anymore.

ALEX. You're hard, that's your problem.

PAT. No, I'm not, and *that's* my problem.

ALEX *(studying the jigsaw)*. You could do the roof.

PAT. Any fool could do the roof. But there's nowhere to put the roof, except on the top of the wall and I haven't done the wall because the wall is the same boring colour as the street and the sky and the fence and the sea. What sadistic bastard invented these things, anyway?

ALEX. Leave it alone.

PAT. I'm not a quitter, Alex. I can do this. It just might take me several centuries.

ALEX. What's the point? What are you trying to prove? Remember, jigsaws are supposed to be fun.

PAT. I'm having a wonderful time.

ALEX. I can tell. *(Glancing at her watch.)* Would you mind if I made a quick phone call?

PAT. Go ahead. *(Pause. ALEX makes no move.)* Oh, it's someone special?

ALEX. Yes, it is.

PAT. I hope he's not like the last one. Your mother was on the phone to Sydney every two minutes trying to convince me you were about to be swept off into a commune of non-stop orgies.

ALEX. What did you say?

PAT. I asked for his address.

ALEX. This is different.

PAT. Did he go to a good school? Does he know the right people? Does he make enough money? That's all your mother will want to know.

ALEX. She's forgiven Monica for marrying Nick.

PAT. Has she? Well, Nick's crude the way oil is crude. Thick and rich. It covers a lot of sins. Anyway, you don't need her permission. *(ALEX is quiet. PAT stares, her attention diverted from the jigsaw for a moment.)* Is this, at long last, love?

ALEX. I'm afraid it is.

PAT. He's married. You idiot. You should know better. I bet he's got a wife who doesn't understand him, and three children that he can't possibly leave because they're too young and what would it do to them? So all you have to do is hang about for ten years and you can walk off together into the sunset.

(Enter MONICA who immediately begins to tidy. A compulsive housewife, MONICA never relaxes.)

PAT. You're a sentimental fool, Alex. Very smart in many ways, but very soft in others. You're always rushing off into the dark woods to play with the gypsies.

ALEX. Sometimes you've got to take chances.

PAT. Stockbrokers take chances, and then only with someone else's money. The rest of us make decisions. You're the one who's always telling me that. *(MONICA reaches across ALEX to retrieve her empty glass.)*

MONICA. Excuse me. There's another bottle in the fridge. Didn't you know?

ALEX. Don't you think you've had enough?

MONICA. Aunty Nellie has. She's in a dreadful state, out there in all this heat, demanding that everyone plays cricket. I don't suppose you've noticed. Did you see Gran?

ALEX. I've been back for three days. Yes, I've seen Gran.

MONICA. She's looking terrible.

ALEX. I can see she's tired.

MONICA. She can't manage. It's as simple as that. We need to get her settled.

ALEX. Into what? Her coffin?

PAT. Don't start, Alex! *(To MONICA.)* What are you talking about?

MONICA. Gran and Aunty Nellie. They need to be looked after.

PAT. You mean a nursing home.

MONICA. Something like that.

PAT. Mum hasn't said anything to me about moving out of here.

MONICA. She doesn't know yet. Christmas didn't seem the right time to discuss it.

ALEX. Oh, this is Mum's happy New Year surprise, is it? We can all join hands singing "Auld Lang Syne" and shuffle them straight into their padded cells. Pop in a valium twice daily and leave them to rot.

PAT. Calm down.

MONICA. What difference does it make to you? You're never here. You never do anything. You don't call in twice a day, or cook their meals, or strip the stinking sheets off the bed. You don't take them out for drives, or out shopping, or down to the doctors. You're never here when Aunty Nellie goes wandering off, or Gran starts crying. It's easy for you to get all righteous and noble. You don't know what it's like, and you don't want to know. You haven't even been here for Christmas for years. Not even then. You don't know what pills they take, or what they can eat, or how much mess they make. You don't even know about the fire.

ALEX. Have you noticed the way Monica drops these little gems into the conversation, then stops? All right, we give up. What fire?

MONICA. The frying pan caught alight. If Marge, from next door, hadn't been here the whole place would have burnt to the ground. So, you see.

ALEX. Illuminate my thinking.

MONICA. Don't you start on me. Mum's made up her mind and you know what she's like.

ALEX. Yes, I know what she's like. Like one of those giant clams that grab your leg and hold you under till you run out of air.

MONICA. Gran's in a world of her own most of the time. She talks to Grandad, and he's been dead for two years in April. It's time she got over it.

PAT. Mourning isn't like having the measles.

MONICA *(crying out as if in pain)*. Oh, no!

ALEX. What happened?

PAT. What is it?

MONICA. I don't believe it.

ALEX. What's wrong?

MONICA. Look at that. Just look at that!

ALEX. What?

MONICA *(pointing dramatically)*. *That!*

PAT. Where?

MONICA. That stain.

PAT. Oh.

ALEX. Oh.

MONICA. Can't you see it?

PAT. Vaguely.

MONICA. Someone has spilt their coffee and just, left it! What do you think of that?

PAT. I think it's a good thing Mum's got a brown carpet.

ALEX. If you stand over here you can't even see the mark. *(MONICA exits.)* If Monica was a colour, what colour would she be?

PAT. Puce. No, grey. Sea grey, stone grey, sky grey. You shouldn't bait her so much.

ALEX. I know. It's force of habit. When she was six I bit her and she ran screaming to Mum. It's been the pattern ever since.

(Enter MONICA with cloths to clean up the coffee stain.)

MONICA. Accidents happen. We all know that. Anyone can spill something. But not to clean it up! I can't understand that sort of mentality.

PAT. It's probably been there for months.

MONICA. I clean this room. Every week. Thoroughly.

PAT. Someone was careless.

MONICA. Careless? Is that what you call it? It's sluttish. That's what it is.

ALEX. What a lovely word. Sluttish. Sluttish and proud of it. Miss Sluttish, 1987. After the crowning ceremony the revolting winner had this to say: "I never knew I could sink this low. It's all due to my repulsive Mum who set such a filthy example. It really depressed me into doing my worst." *(There is the sound of a tennis ball hitting the window. PAT crosses to the window and opens it. Voices off.)*

PAT. Okay, we're coming out. Anyone for cricket? The sea breeze is in. We'd better go and keep Aunty Nellie happy. You coming?

ALEX. I'd like to make that call.

PAT. If you must. Don't say I didn't warn you. What about you Monica?

MONICA. There's work to be done.

PAT. Ah, well, no rest for the wicked.

MONICA. In my experience the wicked do very well for themselves. *(Reaching over and fitting in a piece of jigsaw.)* These are really relaxing, aren't they? *(PAT exits. MONICA continues to work on the jigsaw.)* Don't forget your phone call. Eastern states, is it? Or overseas? You haven't got any friends here these days, have you? Well, you're away so much. All that travelling. It must be exhausting. I suppose you need to drink, to get through it all. *(Pause.)* I hear you're buying a house with a friend. What's the attraction in Melbourne?

ALEX. I am moving to Melbourne because of my job. I travel because of my job. Those are facts, not sins.

MONICA. But you enjoy it.

ALEX. When it gives me emotional satisfaction, creative achievement, and a handsome financial reward, yes. On the other hand, when it offers physical exhaustion, mental disintegration, and a large dose of paranoia, then no, I don't.

MONICA. Why did you have to say that, about the lavatory seat?

ALEX. What incisive comment of mine was that?

MONICA. You told Aunty Pat my house was so clean you could eat lunch off the lavatory seat.

ALEX. Did I? Well, it's the truth. The cleaners, deodorisers and sprays in your house have destroyed a sizeable hunk of the ozone layer. Your house is so sterile you could volunteer it for open heart operations.

MONICA. Not everybody likes filth, Alex. I've seen your flat. You don't wash up till you've used every clean dish in the place. You write yourself memos in the dust on the hall table. If you fall down you're lucky not to suffocate. It's a tip!

ALEX. I prefer to think of it as a comfortable confusion.

MONICA. Why did you bother coming back?

ALEX. I missed your stimulating conversation. What shall we talk about next? The price of baked beans?

MONICA. Why don't you pack your smart mouth and fly off somewhere glamorous and leave the peasants to get on without you. You waltz in, and make trouble. You upset Dad because you're not here and he wants you to be. You upset Mum because you *are* here. You needle Nick. You dazzle the kids. You're all over Gran like a rash and then you dash off again. Someone's got to get on with ordinary things while you're out there being important. Excuse me, but *I* have work to do. *(Exit MONICA.)*

ALEX *(closing her eyes and reciting slowly)*. "All women are my sisters, flesh of my flesh, blood of my blood, sacred, singular, unique. I am no more, I am no less than any other." It's all so simple until I walk back through my own front door. (ALEX phones long distance—ten digits.) Hello. May I speak to Diana Collins, please. Yes, it is. Happy Christmas. Is it? It's very hot here too. Thank you. I'll hold. Hello, Diana? Merry Christmas darling. How's it going? Oh, like every other Christmas I've ever known. Thirty minutes of happiness, four hours of boredom, and then the distinctive sound of old grievances being tightened like thumb screws. No, I haven't told her about us. Not yet. I know we said we would be honest, open and proud. How do you feel about being deceitful, secretive and mysterious instead? I'm not chickening out on you. It's my mother. You haven't met her, my love. She's like an express train, racing downhill, without any brakes. I just don't want to be tied on the line in front of her, that's all. You can't talk to her. The best you can hope for is open negotiations. Yes, I have to tell her. Why do I have to tell her? Couldn't I let her guess? I have a reputation for ruining Christmas. I thought I might do something different this year. No, I haven't told Dad. I think I'd have to explain it to him first. Besides, he is really down since he lost his job, and I...

(EMMA enters.)

ALEX *(continues)*. I must go now. Yes. I'll ring tomorrow night. Yes, I do. I love you. *(She hangs up.)* Shouldn't you be resting?

EMMA. I'd rather talk to you. *(She studies ALEX for a moment.)*

ALEX. Are you managing all right? What about Aunty Nellie?

EMMA. She's no worse than she's been before.

ALEX. Mum told me she threatened some children.

EMMA. She waved her walking stick at them, that's all. They were laughing at her. She was shambling round the garden and her legs were giving her a lot of pain. She was wearing her red hat. It sits on her head like a glacé cherry on a cupcake. I suppose she did look funny. She used to be lovely. No one remembers now but me. She was as slim as a pencil, with those huge blue eyes and a mass of auburn hair. It made you stop, seeing her walk into a room. She was stunning. Then the war came and Alan was killed in Singapore. She was never the same after that.

ALEX. She's still pretty lively sometimes.

EMMA. Not like she was. You could have floodlit the Nullarbor with her smile. It was something to see. Never mind, what about this house? Tell me about it. You said it was old and a wreck and that's all you've said.

ALEX. It's a mess, but that's why we can afford it. We think the original house goes back to 1890, maybe earlier, but it's been mangled and mauled so much it's hard to tell.

EMMA. What about the garden?

ALEX. Just as bad. All overgrown and full of rubbish.

EMMA. It's a big commitment. I'm not sure you realise that. I remember when we bought this place, Harry had to borrow two hundred pounds from the bank. He was very worried. Never really slept till it was all paid back. Are you borrowing?

ALEX. We have to.

EMMA. More than two hundred pounds, I suppose?

ALEX. A bit more than that.

EMMA. It's a big responsibility. Women never used to have worries like that, did they? Still, that's progress for you.

(Enter SYLVIA.)

SYLVIA. I should have known you'd find the coolest spot in the place, Alex. Just like a cat—curl up and forget about everyone else. It's a furnace out there, Mum. You mustn't go outside.

EMMA. I wasn't going to. Was I?

SYLVIA *(at window)*. Ian, Ian. Put your hat on. Your hat! It's scorching out there. He'll get sunstroke. Geoffrey, get out of that tree. How can you play cricket in a tree? They shouldn't be playing at all. Get down, you silly boy. Now. Not that way. Get up. You didn't hurt yourself. She must be unhinged. Mother, Pat's out there playing cricket.

EMMA. I expect she knows what she's doing.

SYLVIA. She never has. Stupid woman. She'll have a heart attack next. It's the sort of selfish thing Pat would do. Then I'll have to phone Sydney and tell Ken. "How's Pat?" 'Well, she spent the afternoon chasing a tennis ball round the backyard in thirty-four degrees, and now she's dead.' Wonderful. He would be pleased.

ALEX. She's not dead yet.

SYLVIA. It's only a matter of time. She wouldn't be out there if she'd stayed sober.

ALEX. Come on. She only had a couple of glasses of wine.

SYLVIA. I'm not going to argue with you, but she had four glasses of champagne, and at least two glasses of riesling. Why you had to bring so much alcohol I do not understand.

ALEX. You asked me to bring wine.

SYLVIA. Not a case of it. You're clearly used to heavy drinking. I suppose advertising people do a lot of that. You wouldn't want to be left out of the crowd, would you?

ALEX. I didn't see you refusing any.

SYLVIA. I've been taught not to make a fuss.

ALEX. How considerate.

SYLVIA. Heavy drinking is not sophisticated.

EMMA. Nellie enjoyed it.

SYLVIA. Aunty Nellie is drunk. She's out there now pretending to umpire the cricket. Ridiculous! She keeps shouting "Howzat" and telling people they're out because they hit the fence. The fence shouldn't be out. The fence should be four runs. But no, she won't listen. Your father has batted seven times so far. Aunty Nellie is not responsible for her actions. She must be put somewhere safe. *(A ball strikes a window.)* Stop that! Who hit that ball? Chloe, you're out. Anyone who hits the windows is out. Go on, walk. You're out. I must speak to Monica about that girl. Her attitude leaves a great deal to be desired. I blame the schools. No discipline. Too busy being creative and meaningful, whatever that means.

ALEX. Hang 'em and flog 'em.

SYLVIA. You can mock. The State system is a disgrace. Thank heavens we didn't have to use it. *(Drawing ALEX aside.)* You've been upsetting Monica again. Was that absolutely necessary?

ALEX. No, purely voluntary.

(Enter PAT. She is carrying a bottle of wine and two glasses. She pours wine for herself and ALEX.)

ALEX. How many runs did you get?

PAT. Sixteen. Aunty Nellie decided you got a four if you hit the chook house. I reckon you'll get lots of eggs tomorrow, Mum.

EMMA. Is Nellie all right?

PAT. Right as rain. She's gone off to lie down singing, "Roll Me Over in the Clover." Ian's a bit off form. I hit him two easy catches and they both went down. Is this redundancy thing getting to him?

SYLVIA. It's all a matter of attitude.

PAT. I thought it was more a matter of unemployment.

SYLVIA. Anyone who wants to work in this country can find a job.

PAT. What would you know? You haven't looked for a job in thirty years.

SYLVIA. You don't have to die to have a view on heaven, do you? Anyway, sitting here is not getting the dishes done. *(Pause. No one moves. PAT winks at ALEX.)* Monica's just going to be left, is she? *(Pause.)* How do you manage these days, Alex? Paper plates, I suppose.

ALEX. No. I usually eat straight out of the newspaper.

SYLVIA. It's time you learnt to cook.

ALEX. I do very good *Chateaubriands au Poivre et au Madère.*

SYLVIA. That's not cooking. That's showing off. I mean real things. What about your friend, can she cook? I mean proper things?

ALEX. Not very proper, no.

SYLVIA. Is she neat?

ALEX. Neat? Not especially.

SYLVIA. I'll give this arrangement two weeks. You'll drive each other crazy. Two untidy people together always spells disaster.

PAT. I reckon you could have a whole new future writing thoughts for the day, Sylv. Pithy one liners, the kind they put on desk calendars.

SYLVIA. The Christmas spirit clearly does not come out of a bottle.

PAT. There you go again. Now, what's all this about Mum and Aunty Nellie being evicted?

SYLVIA *(hushing her)*. Pat! For heaven's sake, have some consideration for Mum's feelings. Nellie can't cope.

PAT. With what? I mean, if you're planning a bank robbery or getting the ashes back, then you don't stick Aunty Nellie on your team. She is just not the girl you want. But if you need a little crochet work or a good dominos game, then you're on a winner.

SYLVIA. This conversation is not very helpful. Aunty Nellie is not *well.*

PAT. Aunty Nellie has a dickey heart, failing eyesight, chronic arthritis, and one kidney. Now, given that lot, even you might have problems.

SYLVIA. Mum gets confused. She does. You ask her.

PAT. All right, so she gets confused. You get confused a bit, don't you, Mum?

EMMA. No dear. I get confused a lot. But it doesn't matter. I know where everything is. As long as no one moves it. Has Ian fixed the cat flap yet?

SYLVIA. The cat's dead, Mum.

EMMA. Which one? We've had so many cats. *(Turning to ALEX.)* When your Mum was a little girl we were thinking of moving and she cried and cried. She didn't want to go without the cats. But most of them were dead. She didn't care. "Dig 'em up," she said. "Dig 'em up, Dad." Well, Harry really didn't fancy that. You were very upset, weren't you?

SYLVIA. I don't remember, Mum.

EMMA. Don't you? You're young to be losing your memory. *(EMMA exits.)*

SYLVIA. See what you've done. You've upset her. *(Pause.)* Ian agrees with me. He's going to take Mum round some places after Christmas.

ALEX. Isn't that rather like offering a condemned man a choice of nooses?

SYLVIA. Go and help with the dishes.

ALEX. Monica will have finished them. She's probably out scrubbing down the back steps with a toothbrush by now.

PAT. Mum's staying in this house.

SYLVIA. We're not going to argue about this, are we?

PAT. You might. I'm not.

SYLVIA. We should discuss it sensibly.

PAT. I have enough trouble in my own backyard, Sylvia.

SYLVIA. So, Ken's found another woman, has he?

PAT *(laughing)*. Don't be silly. Ken couldn't find a woman in a maternity ward.

SYLVIA. Then what's wrong? *(Pause.)* I was only concerned. You are my sister, after all. I am allowed to be concerned if you've got yourself into trouble. *(Pause.)* Have you?

PAT. Not yet.

SYLVIA. You're not going to do anything silly, are you?

PAT. Define silly.

SYLVIA. Well, running around. Playing fast and loose. Jumping the rails.

ALEX. God, Mum, you make fucking sound like a sports carnival.

SYLVIA. Alex! How dare you! I never want to hear language like that again. Do you understand?

ALEX. I'm sorry.

SYLVIA. I should think so. *(She exits.)*

PAT. It's true what they say. Distance does make the heart grow fonder. When I am in Sydney I can think of her for minutes at a time without grinding my teeth once.

ALEX. We're all women in the same family. You'd think we'd have some kind of empathy, wouldn't you?

PAT. What? Like people with bad backs? I don't see why. Our real instinct is competition, not co-operation. *(She pours more wine.)* Did you get through? Your phone call.

ALEX. Yes, thank you.

PAT *(returning to the jigsaw)*. And?

ALEX. And what?

PAT. Tell me about it. This is nosey Aunty Pat, remember? Tell me all the wicked details.

ALEX. Like what?

PAT. Well, is it fun? Oh, I forgot. This one is serious. Does that mean you're going to tell your mother?

ALEX. That's what everybody wants to know.

PAT *(frustrated by the jigsaw)*. Are there any scissors in here? It's time for a short cut.

ALEX. Oh, just leave it alone for pity's sake!

PAT. He is married, isn't he?

ALEX. She was.

PAT. Did I blink and miss something?

ALEX. She was married. The person I phoned. Diana. She was married. She has a seven-year-old son.

PAT. She?

ALEX. Yes.

PAT. You can carry this liberation thing too far, Alex.

ALEX. I didn't expect it to happen.

PAT. Traffic accidents "happen." Thunderstorms "happen."

ALEX. Now you mention it, there were certain similarities.

PAT. You're not stupid, and you're not insane, so I will put this down to one of your impulsive little adventures. When did you meet this...person?

ALEX. Six months ago.

PAT. And now you've decided you're madly in love.

ALEX. That didn't take six months. That took about five seconds.

PAT. Good grief, Alex, you don't even like women! You find most of them boring beyond belief. You've been carving your way through boyfriends since you were sixteen. That's it! You're punch drunk. Go join a nunnery. Enforced celibacy will do wonders for your appreciation of men. I should know, I've tried it often enough. I know men are difficult sometimes but you mustn't give up on them. They're half the human race!

ALEX. I don't hate them.

PAT. I do. The bastards!

ALEX. Look, men are fine.

PAT. Yeah?

ALEX. Yeah.

PAT. Some of them are your best friends too, but you don't want to sleep with them.

ALEX. I think about it, but I don't. This is a choice I'm making.

PAT. When you were a kid you tried to ride your bike lying flat across the saddle; like a trick rider, you know, with both arms out, and your feet way off the pedals. You bloody nearly killed yourself.

ALEX. So?

PAT. So you're doing it again. Look at me world! There's nothing I'm scared of. I can do it all. Upside, down side, inside, outside. Anytime, anywhere, with anybody at all.

ALEX. Don't be frightened. It's going to be okay. Everything's going to be fine.

PAT. The last time you said that we were boarding the big dipper at Luna Park. You were twelve and I was terrified. You were wrong then. You're wrong now. Look, you're telling me this is a choice. I don't know, but if it is then it's a choice you haven't thought about. Don't you know they'll hate you?

ALEX. Who?

PAT. Everyone. People you don't even know. People you're never going to meet. You'll be different. You'll be one of them, not one of us. Oh, Alex, you don't know what you're walking into, and if you don't know, and if you're not ready, then they'll break you.

ALEX. I didn't want this to happen. I didn't look for it. I didn't even know it was possible for me. But it happened. You can call it a disaster, or you can call it a miracle. It doesn't make any difference. I know what I feel...

PAT. You're crazy.

ALEX. There's just one thing.

PAT. Whatever it is, no.

ALEX. One favour.

PAT. I'm not going to the wedding.

ALEX. It's Mum.

PAT. Alex, if you want absolution, go to confession. If you want understanding, find a psychiatrist. If you want support seek out your feminist sisters. Love whom you like, and when and how you like, but, for pity's sake, don't tell your mother. I know you want to tell her. I can feel it, coming at me like a bushfire. But it isn't necessary. She doesn't need to know. Go away and start a diary. Make it your New Year resolution. Write it all down. I've been keeping one for years. A diary and a vibrator—every woman's sanity support system.

ALEX. I'm not talking about feeling guilty, or ashamed, or frustrated. I'm talking about someone who makes me happy.

PAT. Super doopah. Go away, be happy, and shut up about it. If you tell your mother you're on your own.

ALEX. But, if you'd meet Diana, you'd see...

PAT. I don't want to meet her or any of her friends. I've seen those hideous dykes on television.

ALEX. You don't believe what you see on that thing, do you? The media can make monsters out of anyone. They could make Mother Teresa look like Jack the Ripper if they tried.

PAT. So you're the one who wears the boiler suits and big boots are you?

ALEX *(joking)*. It all depends on what day it is. We take it in turns. Can we stop this, please? I did not expect these stereotyped ogres from you. *(PAT sits at the jigsaw and tries frantically to fit pieces into place.)*

PAT. I don't see why not. I'm just your average suburban aunt. Stocked with the standard suburban responses of shock, horror and revulsion. You might as well get used to this, Alex, you're going to meet a lot of shocked people in the years ahead. I assume this grand romance *is* going to endure forever. Or do you go to bars and exchange partners every few months like swapping a porno video? *(ALEX explodes, sweeping the jigsaw to the floor.)*

ALEX. I need your help! Don't give me this shit!

PAT. Why me? I'm not on your side, I don't like lesbians. That is what you are, isn't it? Or haven't you got round to admitting that yet?

ALEX. I'm trying to work out what I feel, and why I feel like this, and what it means. It's like an avalanche has hit me. It's very tough to stop moving long enough to see what's going on. I'm trying to come out and face myself.

PAT. Don't bother. Get back in the closet and lock the door. It's a lot safer in the dark.

ALEX. Is that what you do? Pull the blankets up over your head and pretend everything's going to end up happily ever after?

PAT. Don't start on me.

ALEX. I thought you were the one person in this family I could talk to without needing an interpreter.

PAT. Why? Because you've been sending me feminist literature for years? I haven't read most of it, and what I have read I don't understand. I haven't got time. I don't want to join the marches or fight at the barricades. I don't actually give a stuff for the revolution, or feminism, or women's lib, or any of the rest of it. No, don't you start preaching at me. It's no good. It won't work. You're like someone standing on the bank of a river shouting out instructions on advanced lifesaving techniques to a person who can't even swim.

ALEX. Don't you care?

PAT. I'm too bloody busy drowning to care!

(Enter SYLVIA and MONICA.)

SYLVIA. Pat, quickly, it's Aunty Nellie. She's had a fall. Don't try and move her. Just stay there. *(PAT exits at a run.)* Monica, you ring for the ambulance, I'll get Dad.

ALEX. What can I do?

SYLVIA. Why don't you sober up and keep out of everybody's way?

ALEX. I'll go and find Gran.

SYLVIA. You leave her to me. You realise Aunty Nellie will never come home again. Well it's all worked out for the best. She's had a good innings. *(MONICA dials as lights begin to fade on ALEX.)* It's her hip, I expect. Bound to be. She won't get out of bed anymore, not at her age. It's only a matter of time.

ALEX. Howzat. You hit the window and you're out. You hit the floor and you're dead.

MONICA. Hello? Ambulance, please. This is an emergency.

SYLVIA. Gran can't expect to look after herself. She'll be on her own. Still, we'll do what we can, until things get themselves sorted out.

ALEX *(reciting)*. "All women are my sisters..."

SYLVIA. Not making any sense as usual, are you Alex? You'd better sit down before you fall down. You never were the sort of person we could depend on. *(SYLVIA exits. MONICA is still on the phone but inaudible.)*

ALEX. You know what terrifies me most? One morning I'm going to wake up and look in the mirror, and there she'll be, staring straight back at me. *(Lights fade, except on ALEX as music comes up: Judy Garland singing "Have Yourself a Merry Little Christmas." Lights fade to black.)*

SCENE TWO

SCENE: *Three months later, mid-morning. PAT is dusting. SYLVIA is on the phone.*

SYLVIA. She must ring me as soon as she gets in. There's been a death in the family. Her great aunt, if you must know. Thank you so much. *(She hangs up.)* What an impossible woman. Said: "Not unexpected then." Good voice though, well spoken. Wonder where she went to school. *(She crosses to the window.)* It's going to rain. I knew it would. I told Ian first thing this morning, but he insisted on going off to play golf. Did you see him hacking at the hedges yesterday? Like a madman. I told him: 'It's not the garden's fault you're still unemployed.'

PAT. Sylv?

SYLVIA. He doesn't listen anymore. No one does. Look at Alex. I've rung her four times in the past two days to tell her about the funeral arrangements and she refuses to get in touch. Do you think she'll ever find somebody sensible? I always thought Robert Dettman was a real possibility. He was the one who had the Porsche, with too many teeth.

PAT. I'd like to talk about Ken.

SYLVIA. Nothing a good dentist couldn't fix. What do you think about the furniture? Should we sell the lot or split it up? I suppose most of it is rubbish. The agent was impressed with the ceilings, though.

PAT. What agent?

SYLVIA. Didn't I tell you? We popped in yesterday while you were out with Mum. You can see how frail she is. I doubt she'll get through the funeral. I don't know how she's kept going these past few months. No one expected Aunty Nellie to hang on for so long.

PAT. I thought it was a tribute to modern medicine, not to her will power.

SYLVIA. Mum shouldn't go to the funeral. Couldn't you make her stay at home?

PAT. Nellie *was* her sister.

SYLVIA *(an idea striking)*. I know. I'll get Nick to video the whole thing.

PAT. Don't you find that idea just a tiny bit tasteless?

SYLVIA. Why? We'd keep the lid on the coffin. It'll be quite a challenge for Nick. You know he fancies himself as a sort of Steven Spielberg of South Perth. He could include a close-up of Dad's grave and Aunty Dulcie's. Perhaps we should go and weed them first. What do you think? Give the headstones a quick spring clean while we're at it. I do hope we can get Nellie buried next to Dad.

PAT. I thought she asked to be cremated.

SYLVIA. Did she? How odd. A burial has so much more dignity. We should do some tidying up. I'm sure Monica would come.

PAT. I'm thinking about leaving Ken.

SYLVIA. We could put some fresh flowers—what?

PAT. I don't know why I told you. It seems like a commitment, now that I've said it out loud.

SYLVIA. Ken doesn't know? You're just going to go back, open the door and say, "I'm leaving." Poor Ken. He'll be devastated.

PAT. What about me?

SYLVIA. You'll be all right. But you know what men are like. How will he manage?

PAT. Day to day, like the rest of us. You're incredible. For years you've been saying what a hopeless bugger Ken is, and now you're worried that he's going to have to tie his own shoelaces for a change.

SYLVIA. I have *never* described Ken as a bugger. Hopeless, yes. All he ever seems to think of is his garage, the sports results and beer, but there's plenty like that. He's not the worst by any means. And he's never left you and the boys in the lurch, has he? What has he ever done that was so terrible? Has he ever hit you?

PAT. No.

SYLVIA. Or the boys? Or run off with someone else? Or failed to pay the bills? Eventually. You told me you once threw a whole roast dinner at him. Didn't you? So it's not all been one-sided. You should think about that.

PAT. I've done a lot of thinking.

SYLVIA. What will the boys feel about this?

PAT. The boys are grown men with wives and families of their own. They won't be devastated at all.

SYLVIA. Ken will suffer. I suppose that's what you want. I didn't like him. I admit that. I still don't. He's always making silly jokes and he drinks too much. You seemed to get along fairly well, most of the time. You didn't seem to be that miserable.

PAT. There were a few rows. Not many, really. I don't like rows. There were a lot of days we barely said a word. Sometimes he'd slam the door and go off and get drunk. But there weren't many fights. At first he wouldn't stop to argue, and then I gave up trying to make him. I think if it had been more miserable it might have been happier. There was no light, no colour, no flashes of fire, just a great, grey, boring dullness. Like a very long, grey, concrete tunnel. An empty, predictable sameness, day after day after day. That's what I'm leaving. The monotony. It was so bloody boring. It was so bloody pointless.

SYLVIA. Marriage isn't some kind of summer fun fair with a merry-go-round and a ferris wheel and coloured lights all the time. It's routine. That's what it is. Do you think I don't get bored? Do you think Ian doesn't get bored? But we manage.

PAT. I'm sick of managing.

SYLVIA. That's what marriage is.

PAT. No. It's what your marriage is. And what mine was. But no more. Not for me.

SYLVIA. It's very sudden.

PAT. Yeah. It's only taken me twenty-five years to make up my mind. *(Pause.)* Do you know that Ken never once, not once, gave me an orgasm?

SYLVIA. He gave you a fur coat.

PAT *(laughing)*. Don't you think a lifetime of good sex would be better?

SYLVIA *(considering the question)*. I don't know. Sex is very overrated. Sex, sex, sex, that's all you hear. People go on and on.

PAT. And on and on and on. I know. Lucky devils.

SYLVIA. You haven't any remorse, have you?

PAT. Remorse? Oh, yes. I'm sorry for a lot of things. Starting with the words "I will."

SYLVIA. Ken won't understand what went wrong.

PAT. It didn't go wrong. I've been trying to tell you, Sylvia. It never went bloody right.

SYLVIA. You should have told him.

PAT. You think I didn't try. I tried to talk to him dozens, no hundreds of times, but he wasn't listening. He'd tell me to stop whingeing and he'd go off and get drunk with his mates. It took a long time for me to realise that as long as I put clean shirts in the drawer and food on the table, and opened my legs when he wanted, he was never going to listen. Never. Why should he? He had what he needed.

SYLVIA. You sound very bitter.

PAT. How strange. Most of my adult life has gone down the gurgler, but still I should be smiling. Never mind, Sylv. All I need is a couple of Bex and a good lie down.

SYLVIA. It's started to rain. I told Ian it would.

PAT. I have needs too.

SYLVIA. He wouldn't have stopped you, taking what you needed.

PAT. I needed them from him. No, not sex, though yes, that too. But other things. I needed him to see me as a whole person. To comfort me, to talk to me, to be on my side. Not to behave as if I was—I don't know—as if I was somebody who only existed because of what I did. I was the person who cleaned and cooked and cared for the children and did the gardening and the laundry. If you took away all the things like that, who was I? I just disappeared.

SYLVIA. Have you seen a doctor?

PAT. You think I'm crazy?

SYLVIA. It could be early menopause. It's possible. Women do very unusual things when they go through the change of life.

PAT. You haven't heard a word I've been saying, have you?

SYLVIA. I understand that you're having marital problems. I am just trying to save you a lot of grief. Go and see someone. What about a marriage guidance counsellor? I believe they're very good. *(The phone rings.)*

PAT. Hello? Yes, Alex, we've been trying to reach you. We'd like to have the funeral on Friday. Yes, I think you should come. Well, for one thing, you're very photogenic. *(Lights fade to black as music fades up vocal version of "Sisters.")*

SCENE THREE

SCENE: *One week later. EMMA enters. It is early evening and the light is fading. It is raining. EMMA is carrying a tray. She is looking very frail and unhappy but there is a very deliberate determination about her actions. She sets the tray down and lights one lamp. On the tray is a glass, a bottle of pills, and a milk jug. She gets a bottle of whisky from a cupboard and mixes milk and whisky. She drinks the milk and whisky as if it were medicine to wash down three pills and mixes another drink.*

EMMA. I wanted to tell Alex this afternoon, but I couldn't. She's going to be so cross with me. I don't want to go anywhere. Why can't they just leave me here? I'm all right here. I'm not bothering anyone. What do you think, Harry? Do you think I'm doing all right? I know he's not here. I know that. When I came back from the funeral all I could think about was the coffin. I don't know who picked the coffin but it was very big, and shiny with silver handles. It looked so handsome in the sunlight. What a waste, I thought. What a waste putting such a beautiful thing into the dirt and covering it up forever. Just leaving it to rot in the ground. And the flowers, all the flowers by the grave, just left to wither away. Well, you have to do that, I suppose. You have to do that or people think you don't care. I came home and waited for everyone to go away. It took a long time. They didn't want to leave me on my own, but I waited and they all left, and I could relax and just think about Harry. I could see him come in and sit down in the chair in his old blue sweater. He'd read the paper, then he'd look up at the clock, and take off his glasses, and put them in the case. He'd walk over to me and put his head just here *(Patting her shoulder.)* and say "come on, Em, time for bed." I can still feel his touch. *(She swallows two more pills.)* I didn't want to see anyone else. I didn't want people calling in. I didn't want to talk to them, or look pleased because they'd come to see me. When they came I just waited until they went away again. I know it's silly, but that's how it is. It's like living in two worlds. Half of me has to eat and get dressed and talk to people and try to sound sensible and the other half is smiling at Harry. It's not a life, is it?

(She takes two more pills. Suddenly, in the dim lighting, we see a figure in the kitchen doorway. ALEX enters.)

ALEX. Hello Gran. How you doing? *(She puts on extra lights.)* Have you had any tea yet? Why don't we try a curry? *(She stops, senses something is very wrong.)* What's happened?

EMMA. You spoilt it!

ALEX *(seeing whisky and pills)*. Holy shit!

EMMA. Why did you come? I didn't ask you.

ALEX. How many of these have you taken?

EMMA. Leave me alone!

ALEX. Is this the only bottle?

EMMA. You shouldn't have come.

ALEX. Please tell me!

EMMA. Clear out. Go on.

ALEX. I want to know how many!

EMMA. Guess!

ALEX *(crossing to the phone)*. You can argue with a stomach pump.

EMMA. Go away!

ALEX. Certainly. Would you like me to turn the gas on as I leave?

EMMA. Don't ring anyone, please.

ALEX. How many sleeping pills did you take?

EMMA. Six. Maybe seven. If you ring the hospital Sylvia will find out.

ALEX. How could you do this?

EMMA. It's *my* life. Why can't I choose? Tell me, why can't I?

ALEX. I won't let you! You don't have my permission to die, damn it!

EMMA. You think you love me, Alex. Then put down the phone. Close the door, drive off. Say nothing. Just leave. Now. *(Pause.)*

ALEX. I can't, Gran. I'm sorry, but I can't let you go. *(ALEX begins to dial.)*

EMMA. No!

ALEX. I'm ringing Diana. She's a doctor, and she's not going to tell Mum anything. How much whisky did you have?

EMMA. That was full. It's horrible stuff. I almost stopped.

ALEX. Please God she's at home. How are you feeling?

EMMA. Angry. You shouldn't have come here. I was doing very well. No one was supposed to be here until lunchtime tomorrow. I'd arranged for your dad to call. I thought that would be kinder.

ALEX. You thought of everything. Hello, Diana? Yes, listen.

MONICA *(off)*. Hello?

(MONICA enters. She ignores ALEX and her phone call.)

MONICA. Anyone at home?

ALEX *(to phone)*. It's Gran. She's taken an overdose.

MONICA. Hello, Gran, you look tired.

ALEX. Sleeping pills. About seven.

MONICA. Have you had your tea?

ALEX. And whisky. Not much.

MONICA. Why don't you pop up into bed?

ALEX. No hospitals.

MONICA. I'll bring your tea on a tray.

ALEX. She won't go. Can't I manage?

MONICA *(seeing the whisky)*. You really shouldn't buy this stuff for Alex, you know. Ah, your tablets.

ALEX. Yes, yes, okay.

MONICA. Have you taken them yet? *(She takes out two.)* Here you are. Just what you need.

ALEX. Will do. I'll call you back. *(She hangs up.)* Hold it! *(She snatches the pills.)* Thanks for your help, Monica, and good night.

MONICA. What's going on?

ALEX. You're leaving.

MONICA. I'm not going anywhere.

ALEX. Gran's just about to be very sick. Aren't you?

EMMA. I'm all right.

ALEX. Not yet, but you will be.

MONICA. She's an old lady, Alex.

ALEX *(pulling at EMMA)*. With some luck she's going to get even older.

EMMA. Stop it!

ALEX. You are feeling very, very sick. You are feeling so sick that if you don't get better very quickly I may have to call an ambulance to take you to the hospital. Then the doctors would need to know exactly what was wrong, wouldn't they?

EMMA. I'm feeling very sick.

MONICA. I'll ring the doctor.

EMMA. It's not necessary.

MONICA. Are you sure, Gran? Well, I'll just call Mum.

EMMA and ALEX *(together)*. No!

ALEX. She has a very bad migraine.

MONICA. I still think I should call the doctor.

ALEX. I've already called a doctor. Diana. In Melbourne. *(To EMMA.)* Don't sit down!

MONICA. I want to know what's happening. I'm not leaving, and you're not taking Gran anywhere till I know exactly what's wrong with her.

ALEX. Monica, I have three problems. One is that you don't know how to keep a secret. Two is that you are a terrible liar. Three is that I'm running out of time. Let me beg you: Please, go home to Nick. Leave Gran with me. She will be absolutely fine, I promise.

MONICA. I'm not going until I know what's happening.

ALEX. No wonder I used to bite you so often.

EMMA. I'm not feeling very well, Alex.

ALEX. Gran's swallowed a few too many sleeping pills. She needs to get rid of them and drink lots of strong coffee, and she'll be fine.

MONICA. How many pills?

ALEX. Six or seven.

MONICA. But why would she...you mean, on purpose?

ALEX. She miscounted.

EMMA. I get confused.

MONICA. It was providence that brought me here.

ALEX. Jeez, I thought it was just bad luck.

MONICA. Are you sure your friend is a doctor?

ALEX. No, she dresses up in a white coat and walks about the hospital looking important. Of course she's a bloody doctor.

MONICA. Oh, my God.

ALEX. What?

MONICA. Mum.

ALEX. Where?

MONICA. She'll find out.

ALEX. How? You're not going to tell her, are you?

MONICA. I wouldn't dare. But she'll know. She's like one of those machines that measure earthquakes.

When things happen she knows. *(The phone rings, MONICA gives a shriek.)* I told you. That's her.

ALEX. Bloody hell.

MONICA. She knows.

ALEX. Panic is not what we need.

MONICA. She's felt it.

ALEX. Calm down.

MONICA. What are we going to do?

ALEX. Calm down. Now, stop it!

MONICA. Answer it. You've got to or she'll come round.

ALEX. Oh, shit.

MONICA. I can't talk to her, Alex.

ALEX. What about Gran?

MONICA. I can do that.

ALEX. She's got to bring it all up. *(ALEX crosses to the phone as MONICA and EMMA exit.)* Hello? Ah, Nick. Yes, what can I do for you? No, Monica isn't here. She's out. No. I don't know when she's going home. Can't you get tea? Why don't you open something. Like the fridge door. For God's sake, Nick, treat it as a crash course in survival. Grill cockroaches over an open fire. All right, go to the take-away. It's less imaginative, but still. Yes, I'll get her to call you. Goodbye. *(ALEX exits quickly as lights fade down and music fades up.)*

SCENE FOUR

SCENE: *Two hours later. ALEX and MONICA enter as lights come up. They are both carrying cups of coffee and looking exhausted. ALEX crosses to pick up the bottle of whisky and pours some in both cups despite Monica's gesture of protest.*

ALEX. You earned it.

MONICA. I still can't believe she'd try something like that.

ALEX. I think as long as Aunty Nellie was alive there was reason not to.

MONICA. Well, we saved her.

ALEX. For what? Mum isn't going to quit.

MONICA. Why is a nursing home so terrible? She'll get used to it. She'd probably be very happy after a while. She'd make friends, get to know people. It could be the best thing that ever happened to her.

ALEX. It's not what she wants.

MONICA. She *wants* to die! *(Pause.)* If she goes to a nursing home then she's got a chance.

ALEX. She's lived in this house all her life.

MONICA. That's exactly what's wrong! She came to this house with Grandpa. Mum was born here, so was Aunty Pat. Grandpa died here. It's so full of memories it's smothering her.

ALEX. If you put her in a nursing home she'll give up.

MONICA. She's given up already. She's trying to kill herself, Alex.

ALEX. I've seen the old ladies lined up on the verandah. They sit, they eat, they watch television, they sleep. That's *all* they do. In six months she'll be another little old lady sitting around waiting to die. You're not saving her, Monica; you're just slowing it down. *(Pause.)* Couldn't she live with you for a while?

MONICA. There isn't room. *(Pause.)* What about you? What about taking her to Melbourne for a trip?

ALEX. We're never there. I'm working ten hours a day and Diana's on shift work at the hospital.

MONICA. Aunty Pat?

ALEX. She's flying home on Friday.

MONICA. No, she's not. I heard her tell Mum she's going to stay on for a bit longer. She could come here and stay with Grandma.

ALEX. I don't know. She's pretty depressed. They might make a suicide pact. Go out together.

MONICA. Aunty Pat's not going to crack up. We can ask. *(The phone rings, ALEX moves to stop MONICA answering it. Too late.)* Hello? Oh, Mum! It's Mum, Alex. Yes, we're fine, everyone's fine. Everything's great. Gran's asleep. Of course she is. What? Wasn't I? *(Covering the receiver.)* She wants to know why I wasn't here when Nick called. *(To the phone.)* I had to go out, Mum. Where? *(Covering the receiver.)* Where?

ALEX. An emergency.

MONICA. We had an emergency.

ALEX. You had to go out.

MONICA *(to the phone)*. I had to go out.

ALEX. To the vet.

MONICA *(covering the receiver)*. Why the vet? Hello? No, I didn't touch the phone. *(Covering the receiver.)* She's suspicious. *(Uncovering.)* Yes, I had to go to the vet. Why? *(ALEX mimes the answers through till the end of the phone call.)* A dog! I had to take a dog to the vet. With a paw. A sore paw. No, a broken leg. It was more like a broken leg. Well, it was hit by a car. A hit and run accident. Yes, just outside. I couldn't just leave it there, could I? Well, there wasn't anyone else, Mother. No, Alex couldn't take it to the vet. She wasn't well. She had fleas. No, not fleas. Alex was scratching because she didn't like the dog. The dog didn't like her. They didn't like each other. Alex is allergic to dogs! You didn't know that? It's a very recent allergy. I better go now. I've got to wind this up, and cut my throat. I mean, get my coat. Goodbye Mum, bye, bye. *(Both collapse as MONICA hangs up. During the next exchange ALEX gets two glasses and pours in some whisky, adds milk. MONICA takes it almost unthinkingly and sips it.)* She's going to want to know all about the dog.

ALEX. See Spot run. Good dog Spot. See the big red truck. Oh, fuck. What a naughty truck.

MONICA. You mean he's dead?

ALEX. He'd better be.

MONICA. But he only had a broken leg.

ALEX. So? If he was a horse they would have shot him.

MONICA. If he was a horse I couldn't have got him in the car! He was a very sweet little dog with golden eyes and curly black fur. He licked my hand when I carried him into the surgery.

ALEX. It's much safer to bury him. You do realise that if he recovers Mum will want to see him. She'll probably want to interview him. And his owners, and the police, and the vet.

MONICA. He did have internal injuries.

ALEX. Thank God for that.

MONICA. I didn't know your friend was a doctor. You must tell Mum. She'll be very impressed.

ALEX. Oh yes, she will. I'm saving it up, as a surprise. By the way. Don't go into too many details about Spot. When telling lies always keep them simple, and never elaborate.

MONICA. Advice from an expert. Not that you tell lies. But when you do, they're very, very good. I used to watch you tell lies to Mum. I'd wait for her to snap you like a milk arrowroot, but she never did. I hated you for that. *(She drinks deeply.)* I'm like warm plasticine. She never noticed me. The only way I could get her to even look at me was by being sick. *(She drinks.)*

ALEX. She'll be looking at you tomorrow if you keep drinking that fast.

MONICA. More! *(Holding up her glass.)* Do you remember when you staged a sit-in, on the roof? You were only ten. What was it about?

ALEX. Mother being a dictator, as usual.

MONICA. I remember!

ALEX. Every child is entitled to a pet. It's in the Geneva Convention.

MONICA. But why did it have to be a carpet snake? I once had a worm farm. But they disappeared. You told me they had turned cannibal.

ALEX. I sold them for bait.

MONICA. I kept hoping you'd fall off the roof. I wanted to be an only child. You ran away from home four times. Four times! No one else ever finished packing. You were always in trouble. And in the hospital.

ALEX. It was a painful way to gain attention.

MONICA. But it worked.

ALEX. It got attention, not affection.

MONICA. Mum loves you.

ALEX. Like a lion loves its dinner.

MONICA. She doesn't like you, but then she doesn't like anyone, except Winston Churchill and Robert Menzies and she probably only likes them because they are dead. Everybody else is too rude, or too silly, or too stubborn. She doesn't even like Dad. She certainly doesn't like me. But that's all right. I don't care so much these days. I don't like her, either.

ALEX. She was telling me you play golf.

MONICA. What's wrong with that?

ALEX. Nothing. I'm sure it's great fun.

MONICA. Golf is not a fun game. Compared to golf Russian roulette is a fun game.

ALEX. Well, it's very skilful.

MONICA. Don't patronise me.

ALEX. I was trying to be diplomatic.

MONICA. It's too late to learn. You do what you do best. Sit there and look superior. You make decisions—I make bread and butter pudding, remember?

ALEX. If you don't want to play golf what do you want to do?

MONICA. Have another drink.

ALEX. I thought you didn't drink.

MONICA. I don't. Nick doesn't like it. Where's my drink?

ALEX. Where are your car keys? You're not driving home.

MONICA. I don't care. Let someone else sit up and worry for a change.

ALEX. I forgot. Nick rang. You'd better call him.

MONICA. That miserable bastard.

ALEX. You'd better not.

MONICA. Do you think it's inherited?

ALEX. What?

MONICA. Worrying about whether the oven needs cleaning. You don't worry. Your oven is so thick with grease you could scrape it off with a shovel, but do you care? Do you hell.

ALEX. I choose to worry about other things.

MONICA. I had to get up at two o'clock one morning. I'd suddenly remembered there was a filthy ring around the bathtub. My house is *beautiful*, isn't it?

ALEX. Yes.

MONICA. I'm proud of it.

ALEX. I know. You're right to be. But who's proud of you? You work so hard. But what happens if Nick and the children aren't there?

MONICA. The house stays clean. *(Pause.)* What do you worry about? Instead of ovens?

ALEX. Nothing much. World War Three, stuff like that.

MONICA. It's a pity we're not identical twins.

ALEX. Why?

MONICA. We could swap lives. Stephanie Powers did that once in a TV mini series.

ALEX. I think you might have certain problems with my lifestyle.

MONICA. What about your job? Could I do that?

ALEX. You like routine. I loathe it. I love working under pressure. You hate it. I rely on my instincts. You rely on your rules. You're ordered, neat, exact. I'm untidy, impulsive, chaotic. You like long term plans. I like short term improvisation. You're patient. I'm always burning on a very short fuse.

MONICA. Apart from that, we're just the same, aren't we?

ALEX. Monica, I don't despise you. It's just that we live different lives. I couldn't survive in your shoes. Two weeks in a suburban brick and tile with a husband, three children and the kind of non-stop routine you have to meet would have me going ga-ga. I swear they'd have to carry me out in a locked box.

MONICA. It's not that bad. You don't think I could take charge of your department, eh?

ALEX. Right now, you'd have trouble taking charge of a setting jelly.

MONICA. Sometime, while you're home, will you talk to Chloe? I can't. I want to, but we end up shouting at each other. She needs to talk to someone. We all do. You've got your friend, what's her name?

ALEX. Diana.

MONICA. Right. You've got Diana. I used to have Nick, but that was a long time ago. We were friends once, you and me. Now we're just relatives. Would you like to be my friend, or do you like fighting too much?

ALEX. I don't like it at all.

MONICA. You're good at it.

ALEX. Lots of practice.

MONICA. I'm hungry.

ALEX. I can go and get something. What do you want?

MONICA. I don't know. You decide. Anything.

ALEX. How about a curry?

MONICA. Great.

ALEX. Or pizza?

MONICA. Fine.

ALEX. Chinese?

MONICA. Okay.

ALEX. No, you make a decision for once. You tell me what you want. You want a curry? Say yes or no.

MONICA. It doesn't matter.

ALEX. Choose.

MONICA. I don't care.

ALEX. *Choose!*

MONICA. Get whatever you want.

ALEX. Choose.

MONICA. No.

ALEX. *Choose!*

MONICA. No, I don't want curry. No, no, no.

ALEX. Chinese?

MONICA. I don't—yes. Yes.

ALEX. You sure?

MONICA. Yes.

ALEX. Great. *(Pause.)* I wanted curry.

MONICA. That's all right. We'll get curry. That's fine.

ALEX. No! That's not how it works. You make a decision and you stick to it.

MONICA. I was being flexible.

ALEX. You were being manipulated. You as a woman, believe that your purpose, your happiness, your very being depends on approval. Mostly masculine approval, but wider, on all approval. If you choose something that upsets other people, or annoys them, or displeases them you feel a bell go off inside, a bell that is ringing to tell you to back off.

MONICA. Okay. *(Pause.)* I'll have Chinese.

ALEX. Did you understand what I was saying?

MONICA. No, but I was listening. *(Pause.)* Can I have another drink? It helps me think. *(ALEX moves to get MONICA a drink, and one for herself. As she fixes the drinks—with her back to MONICA—she starts to talk and as she does so MONICA gradually slips into sleep. She fails to hear most of what ALEX says. The audience can see what is happening. ALEX cannot.)*

ALEX. I don't mean to bully you. It's about limits, about pushing out the limits, further and further until they're not barriers anymore, just markers to show how far we've gone. You talked about being friends. I wish we could. I'd like to talk to you about Diana, but it's difficult. I told Aunty Pat at Christmas and since then she refuses to acknowledge the conversation. Shut the door, draw the blinds, pretend it never happened. You see, Diana wants us to be open, but I don't want to keep rationalising everything. Why should I have to justify how I feel? Love shouldn't be like that should it? I want to tell you... *(ALEX turns, sees MONICA is asleep. She could laugh or cry. She chooses to smile.)* You always did have a fabulous sense of timing. *(ALEX dims the lights and sits in an armchair with her drink. She puts on the radio. Lights fade to black. Music comes up.)*

END OF ACT ONE

ACT TWO

SCENE: *Spring, five months on. Fade up music: Ella Fitzgerald singing "Just in Time." PAT is in paint-spattered jeans and t-shirt painting the walls. The decoration work is almost finished. The set is flooded with light. The heavy furniture has vanished, the chairs on the set are covered in dust cloths, the blinds and curtains are missing. There is a tarpaulin on the floor, a ladder and pots of paint. PAT is singing, in a highly individual, but not particularly tuneful style, along with the music as she paints. The phone rings. It is buried somewhere under the tarpaulin. PAT turns off the radio and after a frenzied search she finds it just as it stops ringing. There is now paint on the phone. She uses her clothing to wipe it off—not very successfully. Enter EMMA carrying mugs of tea. She pauses to admire the room which gives the audience a chance to admire her. EMMA looks ten years younger. Her hair is now coloured and styled and she is wearing a touch of makeup; but it is not the physical differences which we notice: it is her air of confidence. EMMA has clearly emerged from the shadows, and is confronting life with energy and optimism.*

EMMA *(pronouncing her verdict)*. Much better, Pat. It's looking very fresh, *and* a matching phone.

PAT *(still unsuccessfully trying to remove the paint)*. Do you think they'll give us a new one?

EMMA. I shouldn't think so. It took me long enough to get that. They're into satellites these days. I don't think they bother much with phones. Did I hear it ringing?

PAT. Mum, why do you reckon it's got paint all over it?

EMMA. Was it Ken? That man is spending a fortune ringing you up. The least you could do is be civil to him.

PAT. When I dragged you off to Sydney it was to give *me* support, not give Ken a shoulder to cry on.

EMMA. He's taken it hard, you know, you walking out like that. He didn't expect it. It's really knocked him for six.

PAT *(to the window)*. Jimmy, you missed a bit! Look, now he's cleaned up that corner you can see the gnomes again. Aren't they revolting?

EMMA. Throw them out if you want. Sylvia only bought them as a joke. I think.

PAT. You're going mad, aren't you? You've only been back a fortnight and we've cleared out half the furniture, painted three rooms, and gone through the garden like typhoon Tessie.

EMMA. I haven't got forever. *(Through the window.)* Tom, could you come and give me a hand to move the table after you finish the roses? *(To PAT.)* He's a good neighbour. You don't think he's overdoing it, do you?

PAT. He's five years younger than you are!

EMMA. He doesn't take proper care of himself, hasn't since Marge died. Doesn't eat most of the time.

PAT. He's doing all right now you're home. He practically lives here.

EMMA. Jimmy's a big help.

PAT *(non-committally)*. Hmmm.

EMMA. How old would you say he was?

PAT. Sixty-four?

EMMA. No, Jimmy. Mid twenties, I suppose.

PAT. Something like that.

EMMA. Lucky he was visiting his grandad. Such a good-looking boy. *(PAT gives her a look, but stays silent.)* He reminds me a bit of John. Something about the eyes, don't you think?

PAT. John's eyes are brown.

EMMA. It was more the expression.

PAT *(irritated into a response)*. What are you saying?

EMMA. Nothing. It's just that when you're on a diet you don't bring home a fresh cream sponge, do you?

PAT. I haven't even licked the icing!

EMMA. You look, though.

PAT. There's no tax on that.

EMMA. It's one thing to want something and it's another to know what to do with it, once you've got it.

PAT. I think I'd know what to do with it. What I didn't know I could invent. Oh, forget it Mum. I'm drooling, and not doing. Did Tom tell you when you were down at the tip yesterday Monica called? She was doing her good scout impression: sneaking through the undergrowth spying out the land for Sylv. A granny flat seems to be the flavour of the week. At least they've given up on the nursing home.

EMMA. She's forgotten all about that.

PAT. Sylvia's plotting, Mum. It's second nature with her.

EMMA. Noise and bluster, that's what it is. It doesn't mean anything.

PAT. Sylvia is the sort of person who'll run you down with a bulldozer and then reverse back in case she missed any bits. She'll organise you to suit her. And she wants to sell this house; she has for years. Once I go she'll have you out of here quicker than you can say geriatric ward. I should charge her for the decoration work.

EMMA. She can't force me out.

PAT. It's the dripping tap. She'll wear you down in the end. *(EMMA crosses to the phone.)*

EMMA. It's time she stopped this nonsense.

PAT. You'll never get her over today. It's Thursday.

EMMA. We'll see about that. There's other things for Sylvia to worry about. Ian for a start.

PAT. Perhaps you could get them to take a holiday.

EMMA. Ian's had ten months' holiday. What he needs is a reason to get out of bed in the morning. Hello, Sylvia? Are you calling in today? Oh, bridge, of course. So you can't come over? What a pity. Oh, nothing. Just my will. My will, yes. I was just looking at it. Thinking about one or two changes. In fact I went to the solicitors yesterday. You mean, right now? What about your guests? I see. Very well, dear. *(She hangs up.)* I hope she remembers to stop for red lights.

PAT. You didn't see a lawyer yesterday. Did you?

EMMA. It's very important to get Sylvia's attention right from the start if you want her to listen. She's got to help Ian. He's just about given up. I was like that, you know, until you took me off to Sydney.

PAT. Do you want me to take Ian to Sydney?

EMMA. That's not such a bad idea. But no, you can't. He's Sylvia's husband and she has got to be *told*.

PAT. Ian needs sympathy, Mum. Asking Sylvia for sympathy is like asking a shark for a Bandaid.

EMMA. He doesn't need sympathy. He's had too much of that already. I remember when Harry died everyone was rushing around not letting me do anything. All I had to do was put food in my mouth, go to the toilet and climb in and out of bed. No wonder I was halfway to the funny farm. He needs something to *do*. That's the thing. Keep busy. It doesn't matter how much it hurts, but keep going. Keep doing. Otherwise you might just as well climb in the coffin and pull the lid over your head.

PAT. You are feeling fierce.

EMMA. I'm cross. Sylvia gets away with too much. She shouldn't have let him get to this. I intend making my feelings known.

PAT. Can I watch?

EMMA. Onc of the good things about getting older is that you end up answerable only to yourself. And God, if you believe in him. I know you don't, but some people do, even these days. For years I couldn't do all sorts of things or say all sorts of things because someone else might not like it, or might suffer because of it, or thought they might suffer. First there was my Mum and Dad, then Harry, then you and Sylvia. Now I can do as I please. I've outlived all my responsibilities.

PAT. You worry about us. Don't you?

EMMA. If I do, and when I do, it's my privilege.

PAT. And we worry about you.

EMMA. That's your duty.

MONICA *(off)*. Hello!

(MONICA enters.)

MONICA. You've done a good job, Aunty Pat. It'll show every mark. I bought you a cream sponge, Gran, with passionfruit icing.

EMMA. There goes the diet. *(She and PAT exchange a smile.)* Thank you, dear.

MONICA. What's so funny?

PAT. Nothing. I'm finished. Here, give me a hand, we'll take these off. *(They remove paint covers and fold them, revealing a new lounge suite. A male voice calls "hello" from outside. EMMA goes to the window.)*

EMMA. Coming, Tom. I want to get that table shifted. *(She exits.)*

MONICA *(looking at the new suite)*. It's very dramatic, isn't it?

PAT. You sound more like your mum every day. How's the golf going?

MONICA. Oh, I love it. Really. We've joined the club now. You should try a game.

PAT. I might do that. Perhaps Jimmy plays.

MONICA. You mean him?

PAT. The one with the muscles. Yes.

MONICA. He doesn't look like a golfer.

PAT. I expect we could get him to put his shirt back on before he went to the club.

MONICA. Do you know him well?

PAT. I'm working on it.

MONICA. He should wear a shirt. He'll get skin cancer.

PAT. Got a great arse.

MONICA *(genuinely shocked)*. Aunty Pat!

PAT. Sorry. He's probably hopeless in bed. What do you think?

MONICA. I don't think about that sort of thing. Well, not at half past ten in the morning.

PAT. Don't you ever have fantasies?

MONICA. You mean imagine things? Sexy things? Men, and more men, and black underwear, and iceblocks and whipped cream and spa baths and baby oil? No, never. You shouldn't treat men like sex objects. Anyway, he's young enough—

PAT. To be my son, don't say it. There's a lot of sexually aware women in this country who can't find partners. You know why? Because women marry men their own age, or older. If we married younger men there'd be enough to go around for everyone, and, a lot of very happy people. *(A car horn sounds.)* That's your mum, I expect.

MONICA. No. She's playing bridge this morning.

PAT. Wanna bet? Mum! Sylvia's here!

MONICA. She's got people coming over. She always plays bridge on a Thursday morning. You know that.

PAT. I guess she changed her mind.

MONICA. Mum? Never!

PAT. This is the age of miracles, or didn't you know? Be a believer.

MONICA. She *always* plays bridge on Thursday.

(Enter SYLVIA.)

MONICA. Oh.

SYLVIA. What's all this nonsense about a will?

(Enter EMMA.)

EMMA. Good morning, Sylvia.

SYLVIA *(to EMMA)*. You haven't been doing anything stupid have you? *(To PAT.)* Can't you keep an eye on her? I had to drop everything and come here leaving a house full of guests just because you're getting senile.

I'm going to see that lawyer tomorrow. You're not capable of giving instructions to anyone.

EMMA. Sit down.

SYLVIA *(to MONICA)*. What are you doing here? I thought you were playing golf with Dad. *(To EMMA.)* Have you actually signed anything? I want to see a copy.

EMMA. I don't have a copy.

SYLVIA. I'll get in touch with Mr. Payne myself.

EMMA. I didn't see Mr. Payne.

SYLVIA. Who did you see?

EMMA. Sit down. Please.

SYLVIA *(to PAT)*. I suppose there's a very good reason why you find this so funny. I'm well aware of your influence over Mum. I should never have let you take her to Sydney. I worried myself sick about that.

EMMA. Sylvia, sit down and shut up! *(Astonished, she does so.)* I am tired of your nagging and hinting and plotting to get me out of this house. So let's clear the air. I'm not going and that's definite.

SYLVIA *(looking at PAT)*. You put her up to this.

EMMA. I can still think for myself. Now you can cancel your booking for the nursing home, and the provisional place in the old folks' flats. Do I make myself clear?

MONICA. It's dangerous for you on your own.

EMMA. Living is dangerous. If you want to be safe, be dead.

SYLVIA. What you need is a valium.

EMMA. Bullshit.

SYLVIA. Mum!

EMMA. I know you mean well. It's difficult to see it sometimes, but you do. I know that. But I am not in my dotage yet, Sylvia, nor in my grave, and I'll get there fast enough without a quick shove between the shoulder blades.

SYLVIA. You talk as if I'm trying to bump you off or something.

EMMA. No, I'm not. You're trying to tidy me away, that's all. I know it's annoying having me cluttering up the place but you're going to have to suffer it a while longer. I've lived in this house for fifty years and I intend to die here, in my own good time, and not at your convenience. Now that's settled let's talk about something that *is* important.

SYLVIA *(to PAT)*. You always wanted this house. That's what this is about.

EMMA. Leave Pat alone! We'd all get on a good deal faster if you'd concentrate on your own backyard for a change. There's Ian for a start. He's drinking himself into an early grave and I want to know what you intend doing about it.

SYLVIA. Ian?

PAT. Your husband. That Ian.

EMMA *(to PAT)*. Behave yourself. *(To SYLVIA.)* You do realise he's on the verge of a complete breakdown?

SYLVIA. It's not my fault he can't find a job. I look in the paper every day. I cut out anything that looks in the least bit likely. I type the letters, I even phone up and make appointments. *(Pause.)* He still might get a job.

EMMA. He might, yes.

PAT. He might piss champagne too.

EMMA. Not another word.

SYLVIA. I asked Nick to talk to him.

MONICA. Why Nick?

SYLVIA. I thought it might be easier. I even rang Henry Fellowes. They've been friends all their lives. But Henry said he couldn't discuss it. Said he didn't know where to start.

EMMA. Men talk about work or money or motor cars or sex. They don't talk about feelings. You should know that.

SYLVIA. He'll get a job. Eventually. He will.

EMMA. What are you going to do if he doesn't?

PAT. Shoot him? *(Pause.)* Sorry.

SYLVIA. I agree, he needs to pull himself together. He's been drinking far too much. I've tried telling him but he doesn't listen. The other evening I was so angry that I threw a glass at him. It smashed on the wall. I could have cried. It was one of those Waterford crystal whisky glasses Aunty Dulcie gave us for our wedding. I don't suppose they make that pattern anymore. *(PAT is laughing.)*

EMMA. That's enough. Go out and start painting the kitchen. Go on.

PAT. And miss all the fun?

EMMA. Monica, you give Aunty Pat a hand.

MONICA. I don't like painting. Anyway, I'm not dressed for it.

EMMA. Then get undressed. Now go and help Aunty Pat. I want to talk to your mother.

MONICA *(to PAT)*. Is she taking something?

PAT. It's the euphoria of a liberated lady. Come on, I'll tell you about it. Sydney's got a lot to answer for. *(Exit PAT and MONICA carrying painting gear to the kitchen.)*

EMMA. Now, what about Ian?

SYLVIA. What do you expect from me? I've done all I can.

EMMA. You've given up on him. *(Pause.)* Don't you think he knows that?

SYLVIA. I can't invent a job, can I?

EMMA. He deserves your loyalty, if nothing else.

SYLVIA *(suddenly close to tears)*. I don't know what to do, Mum. I try, but he won't let me help him. *(EMMA embraces SYLVIA.)*

EMMA. All right, dear. All right. Let's go and make a cup of tea. Then we'll talk a little strategy.

SYLVIA. Strategy? What do you mean? You don't know anything about strategy.

EMMA. I learnt a lot of things during the war, Sylvia. Most of them I do not wish to discuss, now or ever. But one of them was a smattering of strategy.

SYLVIA. Dad was only a corporal.

EMMA. I was thinking of Frank. He was a captain. In submarines. *(Lights fade as music comes up: Vera Lynn singing "We'll meet again.")*

SCENE TWO

SCENE: *A month later. Work on the lounge continues: there is now a print of Picasso's "Blue Woman Nude" on one wall and other evidence of change. PAT and ALEX are hanging new curtains. MONICA is arranging dried flowers in a vase.*

MONICA. It's all very well for you, Aunty Pat, but what will I tell Nick?

ALEX. Tell him to get nicked. *(ALEX finds her comment hilarious. The others do not.)*

PAT. You're going to need his co-operation to do any serious study. He will just have to cut down on his outside activities.

MONICA. You mean, like business meetings?

PAT. Well, no I was thinking more of...

ALEX. His screwing around?

PAT. Squash games. Golf games.

ALEX. Ball games.

PAT. Whose side are you on? I thought you wanted Monica to go back to Uni.

ALEX. I do. I just don't see why Nick is a candidate for canonisation because he's going to learn to use a microwave.

PAT. He's got to be handled tactfully.

ALEX. You're not talking about tact. You're talking about a trade-off.

PAT *(shrugging)*. Marriage is a trade-off. You scratch my back, I'll scratch your balls. That's what it's all about. If Monica wants to finish her degree she's going to have to offer Nick an incentive to go along with it. It's the old carrot and donkey routine.

ALEX. Don't you see that kind of behaviour turns us all into whores?

PAT. Climb off the soapbox, Alex. Nick has got to agree. That is the crucial problem to keep in your mind. Now, how do you suggest we go about it?

ALEX. Monica says: I'm going to finish my degree. Full stop. End of story.

PAT. End of marriage.

ALEX. I'll buy that.

MONICA. You don't understand. You're not married. You don't have to fit around people.

ALEX. All right. You want to study. You need just a little bit of co-operation on the home front. Someone to say: "Okay, dear, I'll collect the dry cleaning, I'll take the boys to Cubs, I'll get home by six and put the oven on. No problem. I wear clothes, I eat meals, I love my children; I can cope with the harsh realities of life at the kitchen sink. It's okay. I love you. I want you to have the chance to find out what you need. I want you to have your own space. I'm not threatened by that, or embittered, or afraid. The stronger you are, the surer you are, the braver you are, the better it is for both of us. I believe in you. Not what you do, or fail to do. Not the roles you play, or the titles you own, but you. And loving you, I want for you all the opportunities that time and health and life allow." *(Pause.)*

MONICA. I don't think Nick'll say that.

PAT. We're not talking about what's reasonable. We're talking about getting Nick to co-operate.

ALEX. You will have to lower his libido first.

PAT. Cut it out.

ALEX. That would be a bit drastic but effective.

PAT. It's all right, Monica. We know it's just too many hormones. It doesn't mean anything.

ALEX. That probably depends on whether you're doing the screwing, or getting screwed.

(Enter SYLVIA.)

SYLVIA. What needs screwing?

ALEX. Nic—

PAT. The end of the curtain-rod bracket needs tightening.

SYLVIA. Well, get that young man to fix it. I expect he knows how to do things like that. A screw here and there shouldn't be a problem. I'm not sure about those curtains. Isn't it time he got a job?

PAT. Who? Jimmy? Oh, he's raising his consciousness.

SYLVIA. Raising what? Never mind. It's probably subversive. *(She looks thoughtfully at the flower arrangement.)* Do you really want to put the banksia here?

ALEX. Nick would get used to it eventually.

SYLVIA. Used to what? *(Pause. ALEX and PAT want to see if MONICA will brave SYLVIA.)*

MONICA. I'm thinking of going back to university.

SYLVIA. How interesting. The last time you went there you got pregnant. I dread to think what would happen now. You haven't got time. This year you were so busy you didn't even get round to doing your pickled onions. *(Chorus of "Aahs" from PAT and ALEX.)* Your father was very disappointed.

MONICA. I need to do something. To have an interest.

SYLVIA. You could take a course in flower arranging.

PAT. She was thinking of study. Thoughts, ideas, philosophies.

SYLVIA. Philosophy? What good is that to anybody? You can't unblock a sink with philosophy. It's not at all practical. It's just another excuse for self-indulgence. I suppose you could do the English Novel. I've nothing against literature. Mary Symons did the course last year and she said it was very challenging. They dissected Jane Austen.

MONICA. I'm serious about this.

SYLVIA. Jane Austen isn't a joke, not when she's taken apart.

MONICA. I want to finish my degree.

SYLVIA. I see. *(Pause.)* Why?

MONICA. For me. Because it matters to me. It's important.

SYLVIA. But you don't need it. *(Turning on ALEX.)* This is your handiwork. *(Back to MONICA.)* Don't worry. This women's lib rubbish is no worse than getting a bad head cold. You'll get over it.

ALEX. Mum, I know you have a mind with all the flexibility of a steel trap but for once could you stop and think. You simply can't dismiss feminism like the flu.

PAT. Let's stick to the point. Monica is asking for your help. I think some moral support might be appreciated. Millions of women have families and go back to study. It's not that strange.

SYLVIA. It's not that easy. Who's going to look after Nick and the children?

PAT. A part-time housekeeper?

SYLVIA. Who's going to pay for this? Nick's only just bought the boat.

ALEX. Oh dear, we forgot about that.

SYLVIA. What about the children, left to wander the neighbourhood, getting into trouble? They'll probably all be in remand homes before they're much older.

ALEX. Watch out. Here come the big guns. Responsibility, guilt, and punishment.

SYLVIA *(ignoring ALEX for the moment)*. What about meals?

PAT. Baked beans on toast?

ALEX. Take-aways.

PAT. Freezer food.

ALEX. Microwave.

SYLVIA. I can see you two have got it all worked out. I wash my hands of the whole business.

MONICA. It's okay, Mum, it'll probably never happen. I haven't decided yet.

PAT. Yes, you have!

MONICA. If I did go back I'd probably find I couldn't do it.

ALEX. Don't be so optimistic.

MONICA. It's not easy. Maybe I can't concentrate, or learn how to do it, or even want to do it.

PAT. Think positive.

MONICA. They'll probably throw me out after the first term.

ALEX. Atta girl.

MONICA. Or I'll quit. *(Groans from ALEX. Even PAT looks disappointed.)*

SYLVIA. It's your decision, dear. But remember. It's very easy for other people to give advice. You're the one who must live with the results. You make your own bed, and you must lie on it. *(The pompous smug look on Sylvia's face appears to be a decisive moment for ALEX. She moves to confront SYLVIA. She is calm, but suddenly very tense.)*

ALEX. Speaking of beds. Mum, while you're in the market for changes in direction, that is, changes in life-style, could I have a few moments?

PAT. Oh, no.

ALEX. As good a time as any.

PAT. At least give the rest of us a three-minute warning.

ALEX. To do what? Put a brown paper bag over your head?

PAT. This won't prove anything.

SYLVIA. May I be told what is going on?

PAT. I'm off to have a swim. Monica? Do you want to come?

MONICA. No.

ALEX. A hell of a time to be decisive.

PAT *(to ALEX)*. You're a bloody fool. *(PAT exits. There is a brief awkward silence. One senses that if ALEX could retract she would, but she is committed.)*

ALEX. There's something I have to tell you. If you could manage to listen without interrupting, or shouting or fainting that would help a good deal. You might want to sit down.

SYLVIA. Get on with it.

ALEX. It's about my sex life.

SYLVIA. Oh. *(She sits.)*

ALEX. As you know I've been living in Melbourne for about eight months. With a friend of mine. She's a doctor. God, this is difficult.

SYLVIA. She's not really a doctor? You're living with some quack who's being sent to prison?

ALEX *(shaking her head)*. Nothing like that. We bought this old house...

SYLVIA. What's wrong with it?

ALEX. Everything, but that's not the point. You see Diana's a very good friend and, well, she's wonderful, and I love her very much.

SYLVIA. Yes?

ALEX. We really care about each other.

SYLVIA. That's nice dear.

MONICA. You're a lesbian!

ALEX. I wondered how I was ever going to get to the point.

SYLVIA. I don't understand.

ALEX. I had a little trouble with that too at first. All you have to remember is that I am very happy.

MONICA. I can't believe it.

SYLVIA. Who knows about this foible of yours?

MONICA. Foible?

ALEX. A small circle of friends. Why? Did you think I'd take out a full page ad in *The Australian?*

SYLVIA. I wouldn't put it past you. Pat obviously knows. What about Gran?

MONICA. She went to see you in Melbourne.

SYLVIA. You invited her?

ALEX. She didn't seem to mind. I don't think she even noticed.

SYLVIA. I assume that means you're being discreet. Please God. Of course it's just a phase.

ALEX. Like teething?

SYLVIA. You've always been a late developer. Now, don't flaunt this.

ALEX. You think lunchtime performances in Flinders Street might be a little obvious?

SYLVIA. Don't be revolting.

MONICA. How could you do this to us?

SYLVIA. Stop bleating. I've got to sort this out.

ALEX. We love each other.

SYLVIA. What did you tell them when you got the mortgage? Do the neighbours know? What about your office?

MONICA. You stay away from Chloe.

ALEX. It's not infectious.

MONICA. Do you know, a couple of years ago I actually thought you and Nick were having an affair? Isn't that ridiculous?

ALEX *(considering)*. No, I wouldn't have called it an affair.

MONICA. What?

ALEX. Nick. And me. I wouldn't have called it an affair.

MONICA. You sleep with a woman.

ALEX. You don't miss much.

MONICA. *And* men?

ALEX. You know I love fruit salad. You know I love ice cream. It's like that.

MONICA. I want to know exactly what Nick meant to you!

ALEX. Vanilla. Strawberry ripple? No, vanilla.

MONICA. Make her tell the truth.

SYLVIA. No one's been able to make her do anything since she was four years old.

MONICA. I'm going to find out the truth.

ALEX. Then you'll offer him a revolver and locked room?

MONICA. Did you have an affair with Nick?

ALEX. No. *(Pause.)* It was more like a flying fuck. *(MONICA slaps ALEX across the face.)*

MONICA. You liar! I never want to see you again. Never! *(She exits.)*

ALEX. My luck is changing.

SYLVIA. You're going back to Melbourne tomorrow. I advise you to get yourself sorted out. An appointment with a first-class psychiatrist would be a good start. You needn't bother to see Monica or the rest of the family before you go. I'll make your excuses.

ALEX. What are you talking about?

SYLVIA. All that is required is patience. You are not a consistent person, Alex. You don't make commitments.

She'll find that out. In six months you'll be with someone else. Hopefully male.

ALEX. I want to explain what's happened to me. I want to talk about it.

SYLVIA. I'm not sure about those curtains. Your choice, I suppose.

ALEX. Please, let me talk to you.

SYLVIA *(looking at the curtains)*. Disappointing, but then so much in life is. Things so rarely come up to expectations, do they? Annoying, but inevitable. *(Pause.)* You have always been determined to defy me. I don't know why. I suppose you hate me. That seems as likely an explanation as any. You are shallow, completely selfish, and totally amoral. I am only thankful you moved to Melbourne before embarking on this escapade.

ALEX. If you'd only meet Diana...

SYLVIA. I never want to see her. Do you understand? *(Pause.)* If you brought her here I would have to tell your father. The shame would probably kill him. *(Pause.)* Those curtains are not right at all. Well, they can be changed. One piece of advice. Don't let this business get about. It won't do your career any good. You'd better hang on to that. You're going to need something in the future. *(SYLVIA exits as lights fade and music fades up female vocal version of "Bye Bye Blackbird.")*

SCENE THREE

SCENE: *Two months later. It is the early hours of the morning. The phone is ringing in the darkness. It rings six times and then lights go on in the passage, the door opens and PAT enters. She has clearly been woken from a deep sleep.*

PAT. Hello? Alex? For pity's sake do you know what time it is?

(EMMA enters.)

EMMA. It's three o'clock.

PAT. Good grief. Alex, it's three in the morning. Well, it's three o'clock here. Have you been drinking? *(To EMMA.)* She's crying so much I can't even tell if she's drunk. It's this bloody custody business again.

EMMA. I'll make a cup of tea.

PAT. It's not going to help Alex unless we try pouring it down the phone. *(To ALEX.)* Yes, yes. I'm listening. Go on. *(To EMMA.)* Why couldn't she call at a decent hour?

EMMA. Alex has always been a night person. So was Sylvia. I used to have long chats with Sylvia about four o'clock in the morning.

PAT. Oh, yeah?

EMMA. When she was a baby. She was a good listener then.

PAT *(to ALEX)*. I heard every word. Now for heaven's sake blow your nose. *(To EMMA.)* She's in a dreadful state. *(To ALEX.)* Sweetie, people always feel terrible at three a.m.

EMMA. Let me talk to her. Go on. Hello, Alex. It's Gran. Calm down. Go on, take a deep breath, and breathe out slowly, slowly. That's better. Again. Slowly. And again. Now listen: Diana is going to win this custody case, and Michael will be with her, and so will you. Believe me. I know it's difficult. But you have to stop exploding like this. There won't be anything left. Diana's only gone back to her parents to give you a chance. You need to sort yourself out.

PAT. Diana's cleared out? Lucky her. She's probably catching up on her sleep.

EMMA. You can't sit up all night and then go to work. Is a week long enough to take off?

PAT. Not if you want to have a nervous breakdown.

EMMA *(to PAT)*. Go and put the kettle on.

PAT. If I do that I might wake up. *(There is a loud hammering on the back door.)*

EMMA. Be careful, dear. It might be a burglar.

PAT. They don't usually knock. *(Adopting a karate stance.)* I'm ready. *(She yawns very broadly.)* On second thought, go away. *(The sound of a muffled shout from the kitchen. PAT exits.)*

EMMA. No, Dad's fine. He's on the "Unholy Trinity"—de Beauvoir, Greer, and Friedan. Women's studies *was* a bit of a surprise choice, but he seems happy. It's driving your mother mad. Now get some rest. I'll call you later. Good night, dear.

(Re-enter PAT.)

PAT. Isn't Tom an old dear? He was just checking to see if we were all right. How's Alex?

EMMA. As well as can be expected. I think that's the phrase I want.

PAT. She should stay clear of the custody case. Her instincts are right about that.

EMMA. Whatever happened to loyalty?

PAT. There's loyalty, and there's common sense. Look, leaping on your husband's funeral pyre was once considered the height of loyalty. But it had rather drastic consequences.

EMMA. She's very confused. Deep down she still hasn't come to terms with this business.

PAT. Then maybe it's a sign that she's blundered into something she doesn't understand.

EMMA. You think she's making a mistake.

PAT. I think she's about to wreck her career, and ruin her life. I think she'll alienate most of her friends, and lose most of her family. Yes, I think she's making a mistake.

EMMA. You tried to help Monica, why not Alex?

PAT. Would you hand a child a loaded gun?

EMMA. You find it all embarrassing. I understand that. I'm not exactly comfortable with the thought myself. But we can learn to deal with that. Diana is a delightful person. Very energetic, and great fun. You'd like her.

PAT. Aren't you going back to bed?

EMMA. No. I'll make a cup of tea. I'll see if Tom wants one.

PAT. Why do you think he was awake at this time of the morning?

EMMA. It's not so strange. Older people often wake and sleep at odd hours. It's like babies. Sleep when we feel like it. For as long as we need, then wake again. Maybe Tom would like to drive to the beach later. It's lovely down there at sunrise. *(PAT exits yawning.)* The sand is absolutely smooth. Great stretches of it without a single blemish. And the water barely moving, lifting and falling very slowly, like a breathing, sleeping mass.

And the sky, like eggshell, like a blessing. It's such a beginning. You feel everything is possible. *(The lights fade to black. Music fades up slow instrumental version of "Sentimental Journey.")*

SCENE FOUR

SCENE: *New Year's Eve, late evening. There are coloured lights in the garden. PAT is alone on stage polishing glasses. She is dressed in party clothes. From outside the open window comes the sound of voices and music. As the lights come up the sound of "Sentimental Journey" dies away. EMMA enters. She is also dressed for the party.*

PAT. Look. Sylv's finally made it. I didn't think she'd want to miss this bun fight. She looks as nervous as a one-legged frog in a pit full of snakes. I don't think she likes you springing surprises. *(She looks out the window.)*

EMMA. That young man's going to miss you.

PAT. Which one?

EMMA. They're romantic, you know, men. Deep down. You can't go about taking great chomps out of them and moving on. You're like a little girl trying a new box of assorted biscuits: crunch, one bite, and you move on to the next.

PAT. I had a lot of hungry years, remember.

EMMA. You'll get fed up with it.

PAT. I'll send you a telegram when I do. "Dear Mum, no more crumbs between the sheets." Tom's looking very smart tonight. He hasn't got anything to do with your big surprise announcement, has he?

EMMA *(indicating the glasses)*. Take these out, will you?

PAT. I wish you'd tell me what you're planning. Still, at least you seem to have defused Sylvia. She's been quite subdued.

EMMA. How's Ken these days?

PAT. Who knows? Been there, done that.

(PAT takes the tray of glasses and exits to the garden via kitchen as ALEX enters.)

ALEX. I see Mother's arrived.

EMMA. What did she say?

ALEX. We don't talk, remember? We exchanged icy stares at twelve paces and disappeared in opposite directions.

EMMA. Diana is going to win that custody battle. She's very confident.

ALEX. I hope she does.

EMMA. All you have to decide is what is important.

ALEX. These days I spend ten minutes trying to work out which shoe to put on first.

EMMA. You've been so unhappy. Do you really think you'd be any more miserable if you *were* with her?

ALEX. I don't know anything. I used to be so positive.

EMMA. You were younger then. The young say yes or no to anything. Mostly yes. The middle-aged say maybe to everything and end up missing out. The old know better.

ALEX. What do they say?

EMMA. They say it's all a lot simpler than you think. They say, "Stop looking over your shoulder. Live now."

They say trust your instincts. Do you want a drink? I'll bring you one.

(EMMA exits. ALEX crosses to window and then to phone. She dials three numbers. She is about to continue, then stops and hangs up. She is clearly hanging on to her nerves only by her fingernails. SYLVIA enters. There is a hostile silence. ALEX exits. SYLVIA looks less triumphant than we might expect. EMMA re-enters with a glass of wine.)

EMMA. Where's Alex?

SYLVIA. She went out to talk to people. *(EMMA gives her a look.)* She can't stay here sulking all night. *(Taking wine.)* Thank you. I wonder about you sometimes. Your sense of morality seems to be slipping further and further away the older you get. Don't you believe in sin anymore?

EMMA. Oh, yes, indeed I do. There's so much evil in the world and so much of it done by such respectable people. One must always be alert. Your country needs lerts. Sorry. I read that somewhere.

SYLVIA *(glancing at a pile of library books on a table)*. You're doing a lot of reading lately.

EMMA. Did I tell you Alex is selling the house?

SYLVIA *(reading a title)*. Good grief.

EMMA. Yes, I think it's a mistake.

SYLVIA *(reading)*. *Lesbians Speak Out. Sex therapy, Alternative Life Styles, Sexual Preferences.* Don't they provide plain brown covers for these things? I don't know what someone would think seeing a woman of your age carrying out these books. Do you actually read them?

EMMA. Hmmm. Actually I'm planning to say something about the sex books in our library. There aren't enough. I had to go to the Family Planning association for the best ones.

SYLVIA. You amaze me, Mother.

EMMA. Thank you, dear. Did you hear what I was saying about the house in Melbourne? Alex is going to sell it. Such a shame. They'll lose money, of course.

SYLVIA. Why?

EMMA. They've only just started on the renovation work. The place is still in shambles, and there's been all their costs with the re-wiring and the roof and the guttering. Then there's all the selling costs. Oh yes, a definite loss. No doubt at all.

SYLVIA. How stupid.

EMMA. I wondered if it was wise.

SYLVIA. You must point out that it's all a mistake. Tell them that property is the soundest investment possible, especially when it's a house as good as theirs. Tell the other woman.

EMMA. It's not Diana who wants to sell.

SYLVIA. Then tell Alex.

EMMA. You'd like Diana. She's good for Alex, and she doesn't stand for any nonsense. She makes Alex laugh at herself.

SYLVIA. How interesting.

EMMA. Who are they hurting?

SYLVIA. I told Ian we shouldn't have come tonight. Naturally he wouldn't listen. Why don't you get *him* to talk to her? They seem to be allies as usual.

EMMA. Yes, I thought he might have a word. Perhaps he could go over there in the holidays. A little physical work to shake up the grey matter.

SYLVIA. Go to Melbourne? To do what?

EMMA. He could work on the house.

SYLVIA. You can't let Ian loose on that house. He'll have the lot down in a week. Do you remember when he decided to do up the greenhouse? I went away to visit Pat in Sydney and when I came home there was nothing left but a twelve by twelve square piece of concrete.

EMMA. I thought he could make himself useful.

SYLVIA. I suppose he might, but only under supervision.

(Enter PAT and MONICA.)

PAT. What about your big surprise announcement?

EMMA. Later, dear.

PAT. Everybody's waiting.

MONICA. Did you see Alex? She's brooding in a corner. Isn't she incredible. Always the great tragedy. Anyone else would be trying to forget it ever happened.

PAT. Come on, Sylv. I'll find you a nice bloke.

SYLVIA. I wouldn't take one of your young men served up on a silver tray with an apple in his...mouth.

PAT. And visa versa.

MONICA. She lied about Nick, you know.

PAT. Oh?

MONICA. I asked him.

PAT. He certainly makes friends easily. What a gift. Isn't that him, over there, behind the barbecue with the blonde? *(MONICA exits.)* What did Alex say about Nick?

SYLVIA. Nothing I could repeat in polite company. Still, I suppose that doesn't include you.

PAT. You're such a model of good taste, maturity, and clear moral purpose aren't you, Sylvia? What a pity your greatest responsibilities turned out so badly. A prissy prude and a would-be suicide. She won't really do it. It's only attention seeking as usual, but it might be a good idea to keep an eye on her. She might succeed without even trying. *(PAT exits. SYLVIA is shaken – and it shows.)*

SYLVIA. She wouldn't. Not Alex.

EMMA. Her depression *is* getting worse.

SYLVIA. Why doesn't she take valium like everybody else? Good grief, she's living with a doctor, isn't she? She ought to be able to get her hands on any amount of drugs. *(She realises what she has said and is frightened.)* Oh, God.

EMMA. Alex was never one for half measures. If she wanted to die she would have done it.

(PAT rushes in to drag EMMA to the garden.)

PAT. Tom said you've got to come out now. He did. Right this minute. What about you, Sylvia? Aren't you going to hear the big news? It might be something important. It's not your will, is it Mum?

(PAT and EMMA exit. SYLVIA is visibly shaken. She looks at the phone, and then looks up a number in the personal directory next to the phone. She is considering her next move when ALEX enters.)

ALEX. Aunty Pat said you must go outside.

SYLVIA. What's it all about? This big secret.

ALEX. Ignorance is bliss. That's what you always told me.

SYLVIA. I get the blame for this failure too, do I? How convenient. You probably curse me every time the milk boils over. When in doubt, kick Mother.

ALEX. You're missing the announcement.

SYLVIA. Did you try to kill yourself?

ALEX. I thought about it. I imagined you going to my funeral. It was raining. A delicious, dreary day. Diana was there. You two met and embraced. I was so damned jealous I couldn't do it. *(ALEX smiles ruefully at her own joke. But SYLVIA is appalled. She turns her back on ALEX. It is clear to the audience, but not to ALEX, that SYLVIA is close to breaking down. ALEX sees only the rigid rejection. She turns and leaves.)*

SYLVIA. It's over-reaction, that's what it is. You've always been so emotional about things. So intense. But it's not worth it.

(SYLVIA turns but the room is empty. PAT enters carrying some champagne and glasses. She pours drinks for herself and SYLVIA.)

PAT. I knew you'd miss the bloody thing. I told Mum: 'Hold it, Sylv's not come out,' but she was in full flow. Did you hear? She's going to rent the house to Jimmy and go off with Tom on a round-Australia trip. They're going to be away for about a year. Up to the north, right across the Territory into Queensland, down to Tasmania. They'll have a fabulous time. What's the matter with you?

SYLVIA. It's these new contact lenses. They're giving me a lot of trouble.

PAT. Don't you think it's great?

SYLVIA. Mum and who?

PAT. Tom. The bloke next door. The widower. You've seen him in here lots of times.

SYLVIA. What on earth would Dad say?

PAT. He'd say, "Go for your life," that's what he'd say.

SYLVIA. When are they getting married?

PAT. Later.

SYLVIA. How much later? You're not telling me that our mother is going off on a round-Australia marathon in a camper van without the benefit of any sort of formal ceremony?

PAT. At least you don't have to worry that she'll come home pregnant.

SYLVIA. She can't just take off like that.

PAT. Of course she can. Our mother is a woman open to life's infinite possibilities.

SYLVIA. While you're open to life's infinite diseases. What with her going off in a van with a complete stranger and you leaping from bed to bed I don't know where to turn. There's nobody with any sense left in this family.

(Enter MONICA. She is drunk but it is not immediately obvious.)

SYLVIA. And don't you start.

PAT. It's nearly New Year. How about a toast? *(PAT gives glasses to SYLVIA and MONICA. MONICA downs her drink in one go.)* Whose game are we playing, anyway? Alex is right. We should have some kind of instinctive empathy. We're all women, born of the same blood. We've all gone through the same experiences – give or take one or two. We should be more tolerant, more understanding. Kindness should be our by-word. Kindness and compassion.

MONICA. I'm going to cut his dick off.

SYLVIA. Not now, dear.

MONICA. He's a bloody bastard.

SYLVIA. We've got enough to sort out already. *(MONICA helps herself to another glass of wine.)* If you want to have a scene about Nick then can you please save it for another day?

MONICA. Prick.

SYLVIA. Control yourself.

MONICA. I'll divorce him.

SYLVIA. Well, you can't do it tonight, so snap out of it. Nick's always been the same. He's never been able to lift his brain above his belt and you know it. *(Turning to PAT.)* How can you find this funny?

PAT. Oh, I think it's a case of laugh or cry, don't you?

MONICA. He's a...

PAT. Dickhead?

SYLVIA. Don't encourage her.

MONICA. I'm going to kill him.

PAT. Hold it! How about some gnomes? Just for target practice? Round the front by the roses. You'll need something heavier than that. Let's go find a hammer.

SYLVIA. Not my gnomes.

PAT. Look on this as therapy.

SYLVIA. You wouldn't dare. *(PAT and MONICA move to exit.)*

PAT. Hi Mum, smashing party.

SYLVIA. You're a mature-aged vandal. It'll break Mum's heart. She's taken Monica out to beat up the gnomes.

EMMA. Oh, good.

SYLVIA. What?

EMMA. I never did like them. Too small.

SYLVIA. They only come in one size.

EMMA. They are a bit silly, don't you think? Little white bearded men in floppy red pyjamas sticking their fishing rods out in the garden. It might not have been so bad if we'd had a pond.

SYLVIA. You never told me you hated them.

EMMA. I didn't want to hurt your feelings.

SYLVIA. I don't know what's got into this family. Look at you, running off with some dirty old man.

EMMA. I've known Tom for twenty years. You can't hide many things across a picket fence. He's not a boozer and he's not a miser.

SYLVIA. Are you going to marry him?

EMMA. I doubt it. Just have a wild affair, I think.

SYLVIA *(suddenly close to tears)*. You can't just disappear.

EMMA. There's you, isn't there? And Pat? And the girls? How am I ever going to disappear?

SYLVIA *(pulling herself together)*. What about this Jimmy character? Why are you renting him the house? He'll probably wreck it.

EMMA. Jimmy's a very intelligent, sensitive young man. He's going to rent out both houses and live here.

SYLVIA. He'll probably have orgies.

EMMA. I am sure I can rely on you to keep an eye on things. *(EMMA exits. SYLVIA crosses to the telephone and looks at it. She picks up the telephone index and looks up a number. She hesitates and then has clearly made a decision. She dials ten digits.)*

SYLVIA. She won't be there. She'll be with her parents. Especially tonight. Or at a party. Hello? Dr. Collins? It's Sylvia Gardener. How are you? Are you? Alex is terrible. Walking around the place like Marley's ghost. Are you living in the house again? Oh, yes, I know there's a lot to do. Yes, I have studied interior design. Did Alex tell you? Interior design, antiques, furniture restoration, Australian Art 1860 to 1920, upholstery, tapestry, ceramics, french polishing, china painting. Yes, well, I find it all fascinating. What stage are you up to? Really. You're not going berserk there are you? I did archaeology one year and it does teach you respect for *layers*. You don't want to rush into things. Mistakes are easily made. Yes, well, Doctor Collins, sorry, what? Are you sure? Diana, then. I rang to say that Alex is not happy. Of course she doesn't know I'm calling. She'd be furious. I just wondered if there was any point in your discussing the matter again. I know she's stubborn. Terrible. Just like her father. But I'm worried. Did you know she's thought about suicide? What do you mean, seriously? What other way is there? I thought I might kill myself, hah, hah? Yes, you should talk to her. Ring back in half an hour, I'll have her here to answer the phone. I *won't* upset her. I'm her mother. I'll let you go back to your stripping. Remember, *layers*. Goodbye.

(She hangs up and sits lost in thought. PAT and MONICA enter like two children back from a naughty prank.)

PAT. I reckon you should invest in a truck-load of those things. They'll do you a lot more good than that muck you're swallowing. *(Seeing SYLVIA.)* Oops!

SYLVIA. Stop right there.

PAT. I've already ordered the new ones. Bigger and better than ever.

SYLVIA. I need your help.

PAT. Say that again.

SYLVIA. Alex is a mess.

PAT. I have never heard you ask anyone for help. Ever.

SYLVIA. Oh, stop it, Pat. Take that silly look off your face. It's not the second coming. Now, let's talk about Alex.

MONICA. Would she like to smash some gnomes?

PAT. Find her a good man. That's what she needs.

SYLVIA. Don't be so limited, Pat. The girl's suicidal and all you can think of is men. She's got enough problems without adding any more. She needs to sort herself out. It's time she invested some effort. She doesn't apply herself except to that job of hers and what sort of occupation is that for a grown woman? Persuading fools to spend money they haven't got buying things they don't need?

PAT. Are you encouraging this business?

SYLVIA. It's nothing to do with me. It's up to Alex what she does.

PAT. Sylvia, she doesn't breathe without your permission.

SYLVIA. She could do worse you know.

PAT. You snob.

SYLVIA. Professional people are more reliable. It's a well-known fact.

PAT. Like what? You mean a fact, like how many tons of salmon sperm are spread in the upper reaches of the Canadian Rockies?

MONICA. Spawn. Not sperm. Spawn.

SYLVIA. The woman is a doctor. Of medicine.

PAT. So was Crippen.

SYLVIA. I suppose if you thought that she went to a first-class school that would make her an automatic moron?

PAT. By first class you mean fee paying.

SYLVIA. You're a bigot.

PAT. Me?

SYLVIA. Certainly. You hate rich people. The thing is that Alex is not going to be allowed to commit suicide. I won't have it.

PAT. It's in such bad taste.

SYLVIA. It's stupid and wasteful. Do you know how many years' education that girl had? And what it cost us? Her dental bills alone could have paid this country's foreign deficit. I am not wasting that investment. You must speak to her.

PAT. She won't listen to me.

SYLVIA. Well, I can't do it.

PAT. Oh, I don't know. I would have thought a motherly slap in the face was exactly what she needed.

(Enter ALEX and EMMA.)

SYLVIA. Alex. Aunty Pat wants to talk to you.

PAT. No, I don't.

SYLVIA. Yes, you do.

EMMA. No, she doesn't.

PAT *(pulling a childish face)*. Naah, naah, naah.

SYLVIA. Well I have something to say.

ALEX. I don't need your approval and I don't want your advice so I suggest we skip the heart-to-heart chat, Mother. I'll miss the New Year if nobody minds. I'm not in the mood for a party. *(ALEX embraces EMMA.)* Good night, Gran.

SYLVIA. Alex! Want to borrow a razor blade?

MONICA *(to PAT)*. Hold my hand. I can't stand violence.

ALEX. I thought I was the cancer in this family, Mother.

MONICA. I wish you wouldn't call her "Mother" like that.

PAT. It's when she calls her "dear Mother" that you've got to get under the table.

SYLVIA. You don't care what I think, or feel. I understand that. But I refuse to stand by while you behave like a fool.

ALEX. No Mother, you've got it wrong. When you spurn the black sheep you've got to stick to it.

MONICA. Spawn. Salmon spawn.

ALEX. You can't stand in the doorway, having thrown me out on the road, and keep yelling: "Left a bit. Take the third past the garage. Watch out for the sharp bend."

SYLVIA. You shouldn't sell the house in Melbourne.

ALEX. All right. I won't sell it. Not yet. Now can I go to bed and never talk to you again?

MONICA. She might hit her. She did once.

SYLVIA. Property is an excellent investment.

ALEX. So are diamonds, oil and gold. Good night, Mother.

SYLVIA. You've been sacked, haven't you?

EMMA. Oh, my dear.

SYLVIA. They found out.

PAT. Bugger.

MONICA. Serves you right.

PAT. Did you tell them?

SYLVIA. I told her not to say anything.

PAT. That probably guaranteed a poster on the staff notice board.

MONICA. It's only right.
SYLVIA. Shut up.
EMMA. Can't Alex sue them?
PAT. Brilliant!
EMMA. There are laws about these things, aren't there?
SYLVIA. Justice must be done, and seen to be done.
PAT. Unlawful dismissal—of course.
EMMA. She's been with that firm for six years.
PAT. That's right. Six years.
SYLVIA. They won't get away with it. I'll call Payne first thing on Tuesday.
PAT. You might get thousands.
SYLVIA. Even better, we'll go and see him.
ALEX *(softly)*. I haven't been sacked.
EMMA. There'll be other jobs, dear. Besides you always said it was a rip off.
PAT. Yes, but a lucrative rip off.
ALEX. I have not been sacked.
PAT. You're not a hypocrite, are you, Alex?
ALEX. Yes, I am.
PAT. There are people—probably ninety-nine per cent of most people—who could live with a lie, but Alex is not one of them.
ALEX. Yes, I am.
SYLVIA. Misguided, but honourable. Yes.
ALEX. No! I have not been sacked.
SYLVIA. You could have said so.
ALEX. I quit.
PAT. Why?
ALEX. It was my own decision.
MONICA. Ho, ho, a liberated woman.

ALEX. Don't worry, Gran. I'm not joining the dole queue. I just need some time to think about things, that's all. *(The phone rings three times.)*

SYLVIA. I wonder who that could be? *(No one moves. The phone rings twice more.)* Is no one going to answer it? Hello? What a surprise! Guess what? It's her. Doctor Collins.

ALEX. I left five minutes ago. *(Pause. ALEX is determined not to budge. SYLVIA considers her alternatives.)*

SYLVIA. Hello? She's not here at the moment. I didn't upset her. As a mother you should understand that I can't just stand by. Well, you have a boy, boys are different. Simpler for a start.

PAT. There's nothing wrong with boys.

SYLVIA *(to PAT)*. We all know your views. *(To phone.)* It's my sister, yes, Pat. She's into boys. And vice versa.

EMMA. How is she? Let me have a word.

SYLVIA. Mum wants to talk to you. *(SYLVIA hands over the phone. ALEX is in a state of shock. To ALEX.)* Stop frowning. You'll get lines.

EMMA. Hello. How are you, dear?

SYLVIA. Let me speak to her next, Mum. I want to pass on a few tips about stripping.

ALEX *(biting herself)*. I am awake.

EMMA. Would you like to have a word with Pat? You haven't met her yet. She's right here.

ALEX. Hold it! May I? *(She takes the phone.)* I love you. I know I'm a pain. And a bitch and a selfish, possessive, moody, shit. All right, a dead shit. But I love you.

(The New Year begins to strike as a click in the hall sounds off the twelve chimes. There is noise from the garden, the sound of singing of "Auld Lang Syne." In the

room, PAT, EMMA, SYLVIA and MONICA wish each other a happy New Year. ALEX signs off the phone call during the noisy celebrations and joins in the good wishes. The last two, who have not exchanged wishes are ALEX and SYLVIA. They turn towards each other, from opposite sides of the room. There is a tense pause. The singing outside ends. They move toward each other, meeting halfway. SYLVIA kisses ALEX on the cheek awkwardly, then moves back.)

SYLVIA. Happy New Year.

ALEX. Happy New Year. *(The silence is brittle. Suddenly, impulsively ALEX hugs her mother. SYLVIA is uncomfortable but she returns the embrace. SYLVIA breaks away first, but slowly.)*

SYLVIA. Are you making any New Year resolutions?

ALEX. I don't believe in them.

SYLVIA. You've got to have plans, Alex. I was just wondering...

ALEX. Yes?

SYLVIA. If it wasn't time to do something about your hair.

ALEX. Mum! *(The lights begin to fade, but less on ALEX and SYLVIA as they continue to argue through curtain fall. The music fades up, a slow version of "Auld Lang Syne.")*

SYLVIA. Why are you always so sensitive? It was only a suggestion. Just because your emotional life is a mess there's no reason to start looking like an unmade bed.

ALEX. Mother, watch my lips: leave me alone.

SYLVIA. Nonsense. What are mothers for? We can always recognise a cry for help.

ALEX. I'm not giving her up.

SYLVIA. I didn't say a word.

ALEX. Go away!

SYLVIA. Don't be so intense.

ALEX. You drive me crazy.

SYLVIA. By the way, did you ever meet Jean and David Hughes? From Melbourne. I had a Christmas card *begging* me to go over and stay for a while. Charming couple.

ALEX. No!

SYLVIA. You can't bear it when someone understands you, can you, Alex? I thought you were supposed to be in favour of communication? Now, let me find my diary and we can start thinking about some dates...

THE END

DIRECTOR'S NOTES